EVENT BIDDING

T0341213

Bidding contests for sporting and cultural events are attracting increasing media and public attention. Yet, despite the cost, size and scale of these bidding contests, relatively little academic attention has been paid to the strategies and tactics used to develop successful bids. *Event Bidding: Politics, Persuasion and Resistance* develops a comprehensive, critical understanding of the bidding processes surrounding the award of major peripatetic events. This is achieved by drawing together existing knowledge on the subject of event bidding, combining this with historical and contemporary examples to enable a critical commentary on the bidding process itself and the struggle for power that it represents.

The text draws on case studies of 'mega events' including the FIFA World Cup and the Olympic Games as well as a range of smaller peripatetic events from across the world to analyse the bidding process and some of the increasingly controversial issues which emerge during often lengthy and expensive bid campaigns. Finally, the text reflects on a range of critical issues of contemporary significance in bidding contests, including the growing ethical and governance issues surrounding the development and award of events as well as the impact of growing oppositional movements surrounding each contest.

This timely volume brings theory and practice together in one place to produce a critical appraisal of a phenomenon with a relatively recent history and is particularly suitable for students, researchers and academics of sports, events, tourism and related subject fields focusing on the strategic and political dimensions of major events.

David McGillivray holds a Chair in Event and Digital Cultures at University of the West of Scotland. His research interests focus on the contemporary significance of events and festivals (sporting and cultural) as markers of identity and mechanisms for the achievements of wider economic, social and cultural externalities.

Daniel Turner is the Senior Lecturer in Events and Tourism at the University of the West of Scotland. His research interests focus upon the socio-cultural exploration of events and sport and the use of such activity to generate economic, social and cultural impacts.

EVENT BIDDING

Politics, Persuasion and Resistance

David McGillivray and Daniel Turner

LONDON AND NEW YORK

First published 2018
by Routledge
2 Park Square, Milton Park, Abingdon, Oxon OX14 4RN

and by Routledge
711 Third Avenue, New York, NY 10017

Routledge is an imprint of the Taylor & Francis Group, an informa business

British Library Cataloguing-in-Publication Data
A catalogue record for this book is available from the British Library

Library of Congress Cataloging-in-Publication Data
A catalog record for this book has been requested

ISBN: 978-1-138-67929-0 (hbk)
ISBN: 978-1-138-67928-3 (pbk)
ISBN: 978-1-315-56336-7 (ebk)

Typeset in Bembo
by Taylor & Francis Books

CONTENTS

ACKNOWLEDGEMENTS

We would like to thank a number of people who have made this work possible. First, to our colleagues at the University of the West of Scotland for the corridor chats, comments on drafts and providing the environment within which to discuss critical issues around events more generally. Thanks must also go to Claire and Wholefoods Supermarket for providing the sustenance that kept us going over the course of the year it has taken to bring this project to fruition – it may have been quicker had the food not been quite as enticing! We would like to thank the team at Routledge for their support in developing and delivering this book project. Finally, most importantly, we would like to thank our respective families: Claire, Aaron, Ethan and Isaac; and Sally for supporting us through the writing of this book, listening to us discuss it endlessly and sacrificing family time to see it through to completion.

1

INTRODUCTION

It is a commonly held view that the toughest Olympic event is the marathon but, by comparison, there is another Olympic event which makes the marathon look gentle. It has only a handful of competitors, lasts many years, is fought out in every continent of the world, and ends with the presentation of just one medal.

(Scott, in Emery, 2001:90)

Bidding contests for major sporting and cultural events increasingly attract mainstream media and public attention. For example, controversies surrounding the award of the 2022 FIFA World Cup to Qatar and discussions over the value of hosting events such as the 2012 London Olympics and the 2014 FIFA World Cup in Brazil are now covered both in academic circles (see Whitelegg, 2000; Shoval, 2002; Cornelissen, 2004; Black, 2007) and in the popular media. Despite moves by event awarding bodies such as the International Olympic Committee (IOC) to reform bidding processes through initiatives like *Olympic Agenda 2020*, host bid teams now invariably encounter well-organised movements from within the wider citizenry raising questions about the cost and impact of these bids (Lenskyj, 2010). Despite growing scepticism about the politics and practices of event bidding, a significant number of cities and nations continue to submit their expressions of interest to host peripatetic sporting, cultural or business-focused events. Furthermore, the cost of bids, even if unsuccessful, can often reach into many millions. And yet, despite the cost, size and scale of these bidding contests, relatively little academic attention has been paid to the strategies and tactics used to develop successful bids, beyond individual case studies of specific events. This book fills a gap in the literature by drawing together existing knowledge on the subject of event bidding, combining this with historical and contemporary examples to enable a *critical commentary* on the bidding process itself and the struggle for power that it represents. As more and more students of sports, events, tourism (studies, policy and management in each case) and related subject fields now focus on the strategic and political dimensions of major events in their curricula, there is a need for a text that brings theory and practice together in one place to help bring critical insights to a phenomenon with a relatively recent history. We deliberately use the term 'critical' here. Our use of the term refers to our intention to analyse the historical intersection between event bids and urban processes; assess power relations, conflicts, social inequalities and the unevenness of urban development approaches exemplified in event bids; draw attention to "marginalisations, exclusions and injustices" (Brenner, 2009:179) in the event bidding process and, finally, seek to offer progressive recommendations for how event bidding processes can be adapted to address the criticisms they encounter.

To adhere to this critical position we examine the rationale for undertaking bids for a range of event-types. We explore, critically, how 'successful' bids are developed, drawing on sporting mega events including the FIFA World Cup and the Summer Olympic Games, as well as a range of smaller peripatetic cultural events from across the world. As Brighenti, Clivaz, Délétroz & Favre (2005) highlight, the number of peripatetic events making use of bidding contests to award host destination rights and the number of destinations bidding to host such events has grown considerably in the last twenty years. We locate bid campaigns within the broader move towards event-led and event-themed (Smith & Fox, 2007) development agendas within destinations, highlighting the historical issues that have shaped the demands of awarding bodies in recent years. In the absence of a *critical* event bidding text, in this book we develop a broad conceptual understanding of the various strategies used in successful bids, moving beyond the case-by-case descriptive approach often found in previous publications. Finally, we reflect on a range of critical issues of contemporary significance in bidding contests, including growing ethical concerns around corruption, and protest movements in the development and award of events. Our aim is to offer the first detailed critical overview of the event bidding process, shining a light on the complex interplay between technical and strategic issues and offering insights into how destinations identify appropriate events, develop bids and manage a multi-faceted stakeholder environment.

Event bidding: Why do it?

In their text *Event policy: from theory to strategy*, Foley, McGillivray & McPherson (2012) argue that:

> Events are of local, national and international importance. They are important signifiers of personal, community, national and globalized identity…A lot is known about how they can be organized more efficiently and effectively, how they can be marketed, how they can be managed safely and how appropriate venues can be selected for their delivery. Much less is known about how ownership of events might be evaluated; about who should resource them; about choosing among competing claims for support; about which other

public investments should be curtailed at their expense; about how they can best be used to assuage social and economic problems.

(p. 1)

When writing a book about event bidding, many of these same questions apply, albeit framed in a slightly different way. So, for example, in contemplating what this book would contain, we wanted to know more about who decides to bid for which events; where the resource to bid for these events comes from; which development priorities are curtailed to enable event bids to be lodged; what claims about the benefits of bidding for an event to a locality are made and on what basis; how bid committees are formed and with what implications for accountability, transparency and governance; and who are the various actors organising and mobilising to oppose event bids. These are just some of the questions we seek to answer in this book. One way of setting the scene is to look at the public pronouncements of those who are in the process of bidding for events or those who have bid in the past, to ensure we have a clear understanding of why bids are made in the first place and with what intended outcome(s).

Who bids for what?

At the international, or global level, some commentators argue that event bidding is one part of a place war (Short & Kim, 1999), whereby entrepreneurial cities engage in inter-urban competition to ensure they are visible to potential residents, visitors and investors. The modern spectacles of large scale sporting events, in particular, are seen as an important means by which cities can express their personality and advertise their position on the global stage (Essex & Chalkley, 1998). Whereas sporting mega events used to be awarded without meaningful competition, from 1984 (and the Los Angeles Olympics) onwards, commercial success and growing media interest led to more 'second rate' cities (Shoval, 2002) joining the competition to lever these events for urban physical and economic regeneration. This analysis is borne out by a cursory glance at the bidding cities for the Summer Olympic Games over the course of the period from 1992 to 2016. Belgrade, Brisbane and Birmingham bid for the 1992 Olympic Games; Melbourne and Manchester for 1996; Stockholm, Lille, San Juan and Seville for 2000; Osaka, Bangkok, Cairo, Havana and Kuala Lumpur for 2004; Leipzig and Istanbul in 2012; and Baku, Doha and Prague for 2016. Each of these cities could be defined as either second or third tier (some may not even reach this status). Even the very act of announcing your candidacy for the world's largest event (the Olympic Games) can, it is argued, bring your city to the attention of a global public.

However, more interesting still is that, vying for a slice of the attention economy, top tier cities are placed under significant pressure to bid for sporting mega events. Again, Shoval (2002) argues that London, New York and Paris, are "fearful of competition" (p.596) from other cities and need to stay ahead of their rivals by bidding for a sports event. Whilst we consider these arguments in more depth in forthcoming chapters, there is a growing trend evident in both sporting mega events and Capital of Culture (UK and European levels) bidding contests to suggest that strategies associated with *becoming* (or emerging) and *maintaining* position in global inter-urban competition are evident. When contemplating bidding for the right to host the 2012 Olympic Games, London did not objectively appear to need additional global awareness or image change, nor did it need a boost to its tourism industry. However, in the fierce battle for mobile capital, perhaps it needed to remind its competitors of its ongoing appeal, and what better way to do so than being at the forefront of the news cycle pre-bid, on award of the bid and, subsequently, on hosting. By contrast, Tashkent, the capital of Uzbekistan, a former Soviet Republic from Central Asia, was an unknown proposition until it made an audacious bid in 1992 to host the 2000 Olympics that were eventually awarded to Sydney. As reported at the time, the Vice President of the Tashkent Olympic Committee suggested that "Of course it would be good for sports, we'll build lots of facilities. But we also want the whole world to know about us in Uzbekistan" (*L.A. Times*, 1992 [online]). Had it been a realistic candidate and eventually awarded the right to host the Games, Tashkent would have had to build all new venues, hotels, hospitals and even an airport. Tashkent's attempt to be a candidate city for the Olympic Games was short lived, but other former Soviet republics better represent the becoming (or emerging) position. Baku, the capital of Azerbaijan, and Almaty, the largest city in Kazakhstan, have both sought to position themselves as internationally aspiring cities, partly through bidding for large scale sporting events. In the last decade Baku bid (unsuccessfully) for the Summer Olympic Games twice (2009 and 2013) and won the rights to host the European Games in 2015 uncontested. It is also jointly hosting the UEFA European Championships in 2020 and won the rights to host a Formula 1 Grand Prix which commenced in 2016. Almaty has bid for the Winter Olympic Games twice (in 2007 and again in 2015) and also has pretensions to host other second or third tier sport events.

At a national level, the becoming/maintaining narrative is also applicable to the contest in recent years to host both the UK and European Capital of Culture titles. For example, Liverpool won the rights to host the year-long European celebration of culture in 2008, beating off competition from more established 'cultural' destinations such as Newcastle-Gateshead. Liverpool's bid strategy emphasised that the city needed the title more than others because it would enable it to become a vibrant cultural place rather than just maintaining its already privileged position. Moreover, over recent years the title of UK Capital of Culture, awarded every four years, has also been used by previously marginal or peripheral cities to attract attention when their other economic levers have been compromised.

Whereas in preceding decades, only the largest cities were involved in bidding for events because they were the only ones with the capacity to do so, a more recent development is the emergence of smaller, less recognisable cities bidding for events (at European or international levels) in order to enhance their position *vis-à-vis* their national competitors. A good example of a city in the UK which has used events (and event bidding) to extricate itself from the shadow of its capital city counterpart is Glasgow, Scotland. Since its successful hosting of the European Capital of Culture crown in 1990, Glasgow has utilised an event-led strategy as one of its main drivers for economic, social and cultural change. The city of Melbourne, Australia, has also been extremely successful at emerging from the shadow of Sydney, to become known as the event capital of the world because of the way it has, strategically, bid for a range of sporting, cultural, business and entertainment events to develop a year-round portfolio. Accompanying an intention or interest to bid for events as part of a strategy to compete nationally (and internationally) is invariably the formation of a strategic function within the city, to enable coordinated action from a variety of actors (including business, tourism, local economic development, sport and hospitality). Both Glasgow and Melbourne have strategic major event functions that compete for future events up to a decade in advance. Beyond the practice of bidding, they also have coordinated, multi-agency teams operating to ensure successful delivery of the events they secure – an important dimension of future bidding success.

At a local level, it might not appear that event bidding carries much importance. Yet, where international (or global) cities are bidding for events there is always a 'local' context (whether economic, cultural, social, political or environmental) that features in bidding rhetoric. Those offering a critique of event bidding often focus on the lack of concern for locality in the way bids are put together and the impact of potential success on the lives of residents, businesses or visitors to the event destination (Chalip, 2006; Paton, Mooney & McKee, 2012; Finkel, 2015). However, in recent years, something of a sea-change has taken place in terms of how 'local' concerns have been brought to the fore and influenced bidding processes for events. Partly, this issue relates to who makes decisions over what events to bid for and in whose name. Over the last decade, a number of cities have withdrawn from the bidding contest for major sporting events, in particular, due to expressed discontent from local people about the merits of bidding, most frequently associated with the burden of costs likely to fall on taxpayers to support the planning and delivery of the Games (Kassens-Noor, 2016). In 2005, Halifax, Canada, withdrew from bidding for the 2014 Commonwealth Games (eventually awarded to Glasgow) largely due to concern at the provincial and municipal levels of government that costs were prohibitively high. More recently, Toronto, Canada, and Boston, USA, decided not to bid for the 2024 Olympic Games due to similar concerns at the 'exposure' of taxpayers to cost overruns, and Rome, Italy, and Budapest, Hungary, withdrew bids late in the process citing similar concerns. Finally, only two cities were left in the race to become the host for the 2022 Winter Olympic Games because of a number of withdrawals, many associated with low levels of public support at the local level.

The need for an event bidding book

As the preceding discussion confirms, event bidding is important at international (global), national and local levels. Bids are not risk-free endeavours, nor do they take place outside political, economic and social policy considerations. The examples and illustrations presented here are intended to provide substantiation to the idea that bidding for events is not simply an operational or logistical activity. Instead, it involves *economics* (that bidding and winning events can lever additional economic activity which will trickle down to those most in need), *politics* (that pooling scarce resources to bid for a range of event types can lead to a more economically successful, socially just and culturally vibrant place to live, invest or visit), (urban) *geography* (that bidding for events can be used as a vehicle to enact plans to transform certain urban places and spaces), and *marketing* (that the act of bidding enables certain narratives of a city to be communicated to a national or international audience). Each of these considerations needs to be subjected to scrutiny from a range of critical, theoretically informed perspectives. In this text, we do not subscribe to what Rojek (2013) has called the self-congratulatory, laudatory and over-consensual ethos of professional event management literature. Instead, like Rojek, we are interested in foregrounding critiques of power, meaning, resistance and history as they apply to the context of event bidding and associated practices. We do not take the view that events are necessarily progressive or a force for good. We critique the 'intercontinental consent engineering' and 'invisible government' (government, media and multinationals) that use communicative power to shape social consciousness (Rojek, 2013). In the structure that follows, we are also conscious of the need to avoid collapsing different event genres together into one, obscuring the very real differences between sporting mega events such as the Olympic Games, the FIFA World Cup and cultural events such as the European Capital of Culture. To this end, we subscribe to the categorisation of events put forward by Müller (2015). He differentiates between major, mega and giga events, based on their scoring across four key criteria – visitor attractiveness, mediated reach, cost and urban transformation. For this book, we are only interested in exploring event bidding for events that appear on Müller's (2015) classification system (i.e. major, mega or giga events), mainly because these are the events that host destinations view as valuable assets and pursue the rights to host them. Using this system, major events include the European Capital of Culture (though it scores less highly on mediated reach and cost) and large Expo events such as the APEC summits. These events, alongside sporting events such as the Rugby World Cup, the Super Bowl, the UEFA European Championship (football) and the IAAF World Championships (athletics) are also peripatetic – moving from host to host in a cycle, and can, therefore, be bid for. We are not interested here in hallmark events or community festivals that have roots in a locale and cannot be moved elsewhere without fundamentally changing the nature of the event.

Event bidding is important enough, at the international, national and local levels, to warrant a book dedicated to its critical treatment. Sufficient cities and nations around the world are participating in event bidding contests for a wide variety of event-genres (sport, culture and business) to make this topic worthy of further scrutiny. Rojek (2013) provides a further reason for this book, arguing that event consciousness is "an orientation to global problem solving that privileges high profile, disaggregated, discontinuous populist responses over fiscal, reformist or revolutionary solutions" (p.112). He makes it clear that exaggerated arguments, media friendly techniques and the like do little to address systemic global problems. He argues that communication power may work to achieve short-term, emotional and economic responses, but it does little to draw attention to "larger issues of dominance, subordination, representation and ideology" (p.137). We argue that event bidding reflects this 'event consciousness' as bids appear to offer solutions or a fix (Müller, 2015) to systemic problems, at the local, national and international levels. We are told that event bids will lead to transformations in people, places, visitor impressions, the urban fabric, economies and even societies. Bids, enacted materially and discursively, promise untold benefits to a wide range of bene-ficiaries, but yet are often viewed as simply a prospectus or sales pitch that might never (need to) be realised. For those interested in how bids come to be, what interests are served in the process of bidding, who is excluded and what reper-cussions result from unsuccessful bids, this text will be of value. We assess com-peting strategies evident in event bids over the last three decades, being careful not to separate the local, contextual and place-specific rationale for each bid city/ nation from the wider (geo) political environment within which these potential hosts operate.

Guiding research questions and structure of the book

Having made the case for the development of a discrete area of study called event bidding, it is now necessary to articulate the guiding research questions that provide direction for the remainder of the book:

- What motivations and rationales underpin event bidding practices, temporally and spatially?
- Which conceptual tools help explain and critique event bidding policies and practices, globally?
- What discourses prevail in the way that awarding bodies design their event bidding processes and how have these changed over time?
- What roles do local, national and global actors play in event bidding processes and what power relations exist that act to include and exclude some interests over others?
- What are the governance and ethical principles that underpin event bidding processes and to what extent are these upheld in practice?

To adequately address the research questions discussed above, the book is divided into four distinct parts, reflecting the themes identified in the title and covering a wide range of peripatetic events. Each chapter makes use of a range of examples from across the globe, from case studies of smaller bidding competitions such as the UK City of Culture to sporting mega events such as the FIFA World Cup and giga events such as the Summer Olympic Games. Each chapter also contains at least one small case study alongside reference to historical and contemporary examples throughout.

Part I of the book provides the historical background and context to the growing importance of hosting peripatetic events and the bidding processes which govern their award. This part also provides the main conceptual underpinning for the book, to help understand the motivations that inform the decision to participate in major event bidding processes, including the role of the awarding bodies and stakeholders within host destinations.

Part I Politics: contexts and concepts

> Chapter 2: A history of bidding
> Chapter 3: Motivations to bid

Part II gives consideration to the strategies and tactics of persuasion employed during bidding campaigns. Individual chapters examine the technical requirements of major bids, the narrative strategies employed to frame and sell bids and the campaigning and lobbying techniques employed by host nations to influence the likely outcome of their bid.

Part II Persuasion: competencies and campaigns

> Chapter 4: Bidding infrastructure: demonstrating technical competence
> Chapter 5: Bidding narratives: positioning through storytelling
> Chapter 6: Bidding tactics: campaigning and lobbying

Part III examines critical issues impacting on the event bidding subject area with consideration given to the growing focus on ethical issues and corruption within bidding processes and the growth of anti-bid resistance movements.

Part III Resistance: corruption and contestation

> Chapter 7: Governance, ethics and impropriety
> Chapter 8: Resistance and alternative campaigns

In Part IV we seek to bring together the themes and concerns of the wider book through in-depth case studies of two very different event bids.

Part IV Case studies in event bidding

> Chapter 9: Rio 2016 Olympic bid: putting South America on the map
> Chapter 10: Marseille-Provence 2013: 'The unquenchable thirst for creative destruction'

Finally, in the concluding chapter we provide an overarching analysis of contemporary event bidding processes and offer comment on the future direction of such campaigns.

References

Black, D. (2007) The symbolic politics of sport mega-events: 2010 in comparative perspective. *Politikon*, 34(3), pp.261–276.

Brenner, N. (2009) What is critical urban theory? *City*, 13(2–3), pp.198–207.

Brighenti, O., Clivaz, C., Délétroz, and Favre, N. (2005) *From initial idea to success: A guide to bidding for sports events for politicians and administrators*. Chavannes-Lausanne, Switzerland: Sports Event Network for Tourism and Economic Development of the Alpine Space.

Chalip, L. (2006) Towards social leverage of sport events. *Journal of Sport & Tourism*, 11(2), pp.109–127.

Cornelissen, S. (2004) Sport mega-events in Africa: Processes, impacts and prospects. *Tourism and Hospitality Planning & Development*, 1(1), pp.39–55.

Emery, P.R. (2001) Bidding to host a major sports event. In C. Gratton and I.P. Henry (eds), *Sport in the city: The role of sport in economic and social regeneration* (pp.90–108). London and New York: Routledge.

Essex, S. and Chalkley, B. (1998) Olympic Games: Catalyst of urban change. *Leisure Studies*, 17(3), pp.187–206.

Finkel, R. (2015) Introduction to Special Issue on Social Justice & Events-related Policy. *Journal of Policy Research in Tourism, Leisure & Events*, 7(3), pp.217–219.

Foley, M., McGillivray, D. and McPherson, G. (2012) *Event policy: From theory to strategy*. London: Routledge.

Kassens-Noor, E. (2016) From ephemeral planning to permanent urbanism: An urban planning theory of mega-events. *Urban Planning*, 1(1), pp.41–54.

L.A. Times (1992) Tashkent's long-shot Olympic bid: Oodles of hospitality, few facilities. Available at http://articles.latimes.com/1992-05-24/sports/sp-149_1_olympic-committee (accessed 21 December 2016).

Lenskyj, H. (2010) Olympic impacts on bid and host cities. In V. Girginov (ed.), *The Olympics: A critical reader*. London: Routledge.

Müller, M. (2015) The mega-event syndrome: Why so much goes wrong in mega-event planning and what to do about it. *Journal of the American Planning Association*, 81(1), pp.6–17.

Paton, K., Mooney, G. and McKee, K. (2012) Class, citizenship and regeneration: Glasgow and the Commonwealth Games 2014. *Antipode*, 44(4), pp.1470–1489.

Rojek, C. (2013) *Event power: How global events manage and manipulate*. London: Sage.

Short, J.R. and Kim, Y.H. (1999) *Globalization and the city*. Harlow: Pearson Prentice Hall.

Shoval, N. (2002) A new phase in the competition for the Olympic gold: The London and New York bids for the 2012 Games. *Journal of Urban Affairs*, 24(5), pp.583–599.

Smith, A. and Fox, T. (2007) From 'event-led' to 'event-themed' regeneration: The 2002 Commonwealth Games Legacy Programme. *Urban Studies*, 44(5–6), pp.1125–1143.

Whitelegg, D. (2000) Going for gold: Atlanta's bid for fame. *International Journal of Urban & Regional Research*, 24(4), pp.801–817.

PART I

Politics: contexts and concepts

2

A HISTORY OF BIDDING

Introduction

Before examining how contemporary event bids are won and lost and considering the motivations that underpin bidding processes for major events, it is necessary to understand what drives 'the will to bid'. Given the significant human and financial resources required to undertake a bid for 'footloose' (Richards & Palmer, 2012) events, and the uncertainty of outcome inherent to the process (Masterman, 2009), what makes cities and nations around the world attempt to win the rights to host major peripatetic events? This question is particularly important in light of the growing critique of the value of sporting mega events in general (Chalip, 2006; Müller 2015). In order to address this question it is necessary to consider the historic importance of events to cities and nations, and to assess how bidding contests for sporting, cultural and commercial events have evolved.

Peripatetic events and the eventful city

The history of urban development strategies centred around the use of major events as a driver of civic enhancement has been discussed widely in recent years, and a clear narrative can be traced across these accounts with events being increasingly *planned* by an ever more interventionist state, rather than occurring at the margins of managed civic life (see Foley, McGillivray & McPherson, 2012; Smith, 2012; Richards & Palmer, 2012). Similarly, a clear trend has emerged in the academic literature highlighting the ways in which such events are used to transform localities, with new forms of legacy emerging periodically (Leopkey & Parent, 2012), extending the reach of events further into spheres such as employment, education and health. Competition to host events can be linked to the success with which these legacies are achieved. As one sporting mega event is considered to have delivered a particular form of positive impact, planned or unplanned, that impact is quickly built into the narrative of future candidate city bids and, in time, the priorities of awarding bodies incorporate these wider impacts into their requirements. The central focus of the chapter is on the evolution of the bidding process and nature of bids for the Summer Olympic Games, as the bidding cycle around this event has, historically, been the most prominent in terms of both interest from prospective hosts and in the academic literature. It has also been, historically speaking, the most organised and managed bid process, with other major events, such as the FIFA World Cup, only adopting a similar bidding system in more recent years.

Early mega events

The world of events and the state, at local, regional and national levels, have intertwined throughout the ages, with festivity performing the role of what Smith (2012) terms 'spectacles and safety valves' throughout history. This can be seen in the 'bread and circuses' of Ancient Rome's Colosseum to the propaganda of the 1936 'Nazi Olympics' in Berlin (Miah & García, 2012) and beyond. Roche (2000) highlights a historical use of events such as Expos and the Olympic Games from the mid-nineteenth century to the present day, emphasising the state subsidy of such events as a means of telling "'the story of a country', a people, a nation" (p.6) and ensuring the construction of images of nation-states in the eyes of the rest of the world. His work highlights the role of Expos and early sporting mega events in demonstrating the high cultural forms of Western civilisation; for they were typically the preserve of Western nations during this period, and he highlights how this ultimately parlayed into an attempt to position the nation demonstrating their practices as a global leader. Krüger's (1999) discussion of the creation of the now ubiquitous symbols of the Olympic Games, the Olympic Torch and its relay at the 1936 Berlin Olympic Games, highlights this notion well, with such practices constructed to locate Nazi Germany as the "legitimate heir of Sparta" (p.14) as the great civilisation of the age.

However, despite the above, the use of events as an urban development tool, delivering a wide range of transformations is a relatively modern phenomenon which has emerged in the twentieth century. Indeed, as Chalkley & Essex (1999) outline, the first three Olympic Games were 'assigned' without a competitive process and, therefore, without the detailed plans for urban renewal which characterise contemporary sporting mega event bids. Hosting the Games in this period was seen as an obligation of patronage for leading global cities rather than a reward or privilege. The Olympic Games, during the early twentieth century, were smaller in their impact upon the host than contemporary events, lacking even the development of sporting infrastructure synonymous with contemporary mega event hosting (Essex & Chalkley, 1998), with little in the way of new facilities or developments. However, by the turn of the twentieth century, this changed with physical legacies being produced by sporting mega events. Liao & Pitts (2006) outline the construction of

London 1908's White City Stadium as a catalyst for the development of new physical infrastructure which remained in the host locale after the conclusion of the event, albeit without the type of significant planning for future use we might expect to see with contemporary event bids. During the same period the Great Exhibitions and World Fairs created physical landmarks such as the Eiffel Tower and Wembley Stadium which provided a legacy of landmark public buildings (Chalkley & Essex, 1999). However, as Smith (2012) highlights, these developments were typically the preserve of the private sector, with the state making little or no contribution nor assuming responsibility for the management of these facilities. The success of events such as the 1908 London Games led to an increase in the number of cities bidding for sporting mega events; however, this number still remained low, four for 1908, in comparison to contemporary bidding contests (Chalkley & Essex, 1999). In the period which predated the Second World War, the physical reach and impact of peripatetic events grew further and began to go beyond basic facilities (Smith, 2012). Dyreson & Llewellyn (2008) identify the Los Angeles Olympic Games of 1932 as being the first to witness a purpose-built Athlete's Village, whilst Liao & Pitts (2006) highlight the Berlin Games of 1936 as being one of the first to develop an 'Olympic Quarter' that included not just a wide range of sporting facilities, but also cultural spaces and the development of civic sites, which went unsurpassed in the years that immediately followed. However, the growing importance of physical transformation, firstly with stadiums and then latterly within the wider physical infrastructure of the host in general, appears to have been initiated by an internal drive within the host community rather than from the awarding bodies themselves. Indeed, there is little literature examining the bidding *requirements* laid down by awarding bodies for events such as World Expos or the Olympic Games during this time. Foley et al. (2012) highlight that, in the early years at least, the only real requirement placed upon an Olympic host city was to maintain and promote the ethos of the Olympic movement itself, an approach characterised as "meaning over money" (p.27).

The post-war period

If the period before the Second World War could be characterised as one of 'accidental physical impact', then the post-war period, beginning with the 1960 Rome Olympics, saw the pursuit of a wider, planned urban change (see Liao & Pitts, 2006; Gold & Gold, 2008; Leopkey & Parent, 2012). This move towards a wider impact in the economic as well as physical sphere can be seen, in part, as a response to the decline in candidate cities for the Olympics in the period following the Second World War (Chalkley & Essex, 1999). Increasingly, the capital expenditure required to build sporting facilities alone saw questions raised regarding the value of hosting major sporting events such as the Olympic Games. This concern continued even after the Rome Games, with its development of a new transport infrastructure, municipal water facilities and urban beautification; and the Tokyo Games of 1964 which went yet further with the addition of housing, tourist accommodation and public health improvements (Essex & Chalkley, 1998). This scepticism led to the first real anti-sporting mega event protest movements ahead of the 1968 Mexico Games (a trend which, as Chapter 8 highlights, has gathered pace in recent years), as student protestors contrasted the lavish spending on the 'Olympic Leviathan' (Lenskyj, 2008) against the exploitation and neglect of the masses by the corrupt government of the time (Shaw, 2008). This scepticism, amplified further by terrorism in Munich 1972 (see Miah & García, 2012) and the massive public debts incurred by Montreal in 1976 (see Whitson & Horne, 2006) saw the number of bidding cities decrease from nine for the 1956 Games, to three by 1964 and eventually led to Los Angeles being the sole host candidate to bid for the right to host the 1984 Games (Chalkley & Essex, 1999).

Los Angeles 1984 and Barcelona 1992: changing the game

The 1984 Los Angeles Olympic Games represent a landmark moment in the history of event bidding, with Dyreson & Llewellyn (2008) going as far as to suggest they saved the Olympic movement. The Games transformed bidding processes, not only in their nature and form, but also their popularity. The purported success of the Games caused a gold rush of candidates for Olympic hosting rights, with dozens of cities entering the bidding arena for the 1992 Games and beyond. Indeed, it is fair to suggest that the 1984 Olympic Games kick-started the contemporary drive towards event-led regeneration across the globe and increased interest in hosting not just the Olympic Games, but also other sporting mega events.

The Los Angeles Games, driven, as Smith (2012) highlights, by a desire to act as an antidote to the excessive debt of Montreal in 1976, moved away from an infrastructure-focused bid, housing the Games in pre-existing facilities and heavily restricting public spending on the Games. Indeed, Andranovich, Burbank & Heying (2001) highlight that the Los Angeles bid was entirely conceived and funded by the city's private sector, with the state a delivery partner, but largely without financial obligation. This mixed economy approach to delivery had, to an extent, underpinned all Olympic bids since the early 1900s (Dyreson & Llewellyn, 2008); however, Los Angeles 1984 represented the ultimate coronation of this approach. With the IOC's position weakened by the downturn in the number of candidate cities seeking to host the event, Los Angeles was, in essence, the only host interested in taking on responsibility for the Games. This allowed the city to push for a Games on its own terms and negotiate favourable concessions regarding the management and delivery of the event. The 1984 Los Angeles Olympic Games became the first to make maximum benefit of selling media rights and sponsorship, and the entrepreneurial approach adopted by the city demonstrated an ability for the Games to be used to create a significant economic impact upon the host, generating a profit of US $380 million (Spirou, 2011). The growth of this commercial agenda within bids has given rise to considerable discussion surrounding its merits and drawbacks. However, the unmistakeable legacy of the Los Angeles 1984 bid has been the entrenchment of a transformative economic discourse as a central feature within major bids.

Following Los Angeles, the range of prospective impacts and legacies attached to major sporting events has grown exponentially, with almost each bidding cycle bringing with it a new addition to the list of anticipated transformations. Barcelona, in 1992, followed Los Angeles in being a 'frugal' Games (Smith, 2012), but rather than being remembered for this aspect, it is most commonly discussed in terms of its Cultural Olympiad. Miah & García (2012) highlight that, whilst many mega sporting events had contained a clear cultural dimension, most notably the 'Nazi Games' of 1936 and the Mexico Olympics in 1968 – which even used the term Cultural Olympiad – Barcelona 1992 represented the first, significant bid to build a cultural dimension into the core of the event. Barcelona pledged, over and above the basic requirements placed upon candidates by the IOC, to stage a four-year, multi-themed cultural programme covering the duration of its period as host to transform itself into a cultural city (Gratton & Preuss, 2008). The event was seen to play a central role in the development of a clear cultural identity amongst the Catalonian population of the city and surrounding region (Miah & García, 2012), fostering a sense of pride and belonging. In addition, as Davies (2012) suggests, the 'Regeneration Games' of Barcelona are seen by many as a high point for other forms of impact. The Games were considered to have generated a profound urban transformation, creating jobs and economic investment, whilst adopting a holistic approach which incorporated a range of partners and stakeholders to maximise the impact of both bidding and hosting the event. Whilst some (see Balibrea, 2001) have been critical of the impact actually secured by the city, the 'Barcelona model' (Smith, 2012; Coaffee, 2013) attracted international attention and became central to understandings of how contemporary event bids are formed and managed. The transformation of Barcelona's image in the eyes of the wider world laid a significant foundation for what was to become a key element of bidding motivations (see Chapter 3) in the years which followed, as cities and nations chasing major and mega events sought to use bidding campaigns and hosting rights as a means to reinvent themselves as attractive destinations for investment and tourism in the eyes of the world.

Contemporary bids

Following 1992, these reimagining and rebranding campaigns increasingly became a key motivation for candidate cities and nations. As Gold & Gold (2008) highlight, hosting a major sporting event is increasingly seen as a way for cities to position themselves on a world stage as a potential tourist destination, or even an emerging economic or political power. Alegi (2001) highlights how, following the growth of the FIFA World Cup as a powerful transformative tool to rival the Olympic Games in the 1980s and 1990s, South Africa sought to host the 2006 FIFA World Cup (failing in this endeavour, but successfully hosting the 2010 iteration) not just for benefits of capital accumulation or the development of civic social capital, but also to actively engage in an outward facing process of nation-building. For a post-Apartheid South Africa, the FIFA World Cup represented an opportunity to reposition itself on the world stage and announce its return to the league of acceptable nations once more following a number of decades as a pariah state due to its apartheid policy. Similarly, Gold & Gold (2008) highlight Beijing's hosting of the 2008 Olympics as central to China's desire to showcase its position as an emerging powerhouse in a display of what Nye (2004) defined as 'soft power'. This trend has continued unabated in recent years with emerging economies the world over seeking to use sporting and cultural events as a tool for carving out a position on the world stage. The roll call of host destinations over the last ten years and in the coming decade includes the well-known BRIC nations (Brazil, Russia, India, China) and a range of oil-rich Middle Eastern and former Soviet states (Qatar, UAE, Azerbaijan). The list of unsuccessful candidate nations has grown ever wider with several African nations (e.g. Nigeria, Morocco) and Asian nations (South Korea, Indonesia) attempting to enter the fray and carve out a clear identity in the minds of the media, tourists and global businesses. In the cultural sector, on a smaller scale, events such as the European City of Culture, most notably in Glasgow (see García 2005; Smith, 2012) and Liverpool (see Jones & Wilks-Heeg, 2004), have also been used to re-brand and transform localities. Whilst rebranding of host destinations is not necessarily engrained into bidding requirements for events by awarding bodies, the economic, physical, social and cultural transformations detailed above *are* increasingly sought as part of the bid process as award bodies seek to see hosts move beyond simply staging the event and create a noticeable change in their circumstances (Smith, 2012). The rebranding process has become an *inferred* element of bidding for major events. However, this wide list of transformations, whilst central to bidding processes since the 1990s, is not exhaustive, as more elements and requirements have been added since this point.

The Sydney bid for the 2000 Olympic Games, as Chalkley & Essex (1999) highlight, sought to position itself as the 'Green Games'. For the first time, environmental sustainability became a key element of a bid, with Waitt (1999) highlighting how Sydney linked environmentalism to Pierre de Coubertin's vision of harmony. Criticism of the Winter Olympics in 1992 saw the IOC under increased pressure to respond to the growing environmental lobby, and Sydney's bid (victorious in 1993) represented an opportunity for the awarding body to demonstrate commitment to sustainable values. Again, as with other forms of impact, the Sydney bid foreshadowed a change to candidate requirements, and Cantelon (2000) highlights how, in 1998, the IOC enshrined the 'environment' as the third pillar of the Olympic movement (joining sport and culture), ensuring that all future bids for the event would have to meet this additional requirement. Similarly, the 2006 FIFA World Cup in Germany became the first iteration of that particular sporting mega event to directly build environmental sustainability into its bid with its 'Green Goal' programme (Dolles & Söderman, 2010), with the 2010 South African version continuing this process (Death, 2011). Similar to the Olympics, as Chapter 4 further highlights, sustainability is now a *requirement* of bidding rather than an option for candidate nations.

The 2000s also saw the growing importance of a *social* legacy for major events. Examining the 2006 Commonwealth Games in Melbourne, Kellett, Hede &

Chalip (2008) highlighted the importance of the *Equal First* programme, which sought to ensure the Commonwealth Games would deliver benefit to all citizens in Melbourne and the state of Victoria, while Coalter (2007) highlights how London's 2012 Olympic bid added a social dimension to the 'traditional legacy rationales' of economic development, tourism increases, image enhancement and infrastructure construction. These social elements have become increasingly prevalent within major sporting and cultural event bids in addition to the economic and infrastructure enhancements which dominated bids up to the 1980s. As Foley et al. (2012) highlight, "it is no longer acceptable to utilise public resources to attract and deliver a sports event, for example, without other positive externalities (or eventualities) being secured" (p.90). Whilst previously, major peripatetic events relied on a tacit assumption that simply providing facilities would lead to a social legacy, the 2000s saw this myth debunked (Whitson & Horne, 2006) and led to a growing sense that event organisers must attempt to 'leverage' (Chalip, 2006) the social power of such festivity if it were to be maximised. Facing increasing criticism that many mega events produced 'white elephant' facilities (Smith, 2012) and under-estimated costs and over-estimated benefits (Whitson & Horne, 2006) in the aftermath of events such as the Athens 2004 Olympics (see Kissoudi, 2008), candidate cities and awarding bodies have increasingly placed host community legacies at the centre of bidding processes, further deepening the requirements to be considered when deciding to bid.

The most recent cycles, particularly those surrounding the Olympic Games, have seen the above issues enshrined within the process of bidding. As will be discussed in more detail later in this book, 2014 saw the introduction of *Olympic Agenda 2020* by the IOC in an attempt to make the Olympic Games in general, and its bidding processes specifically, more sustainable and less resource intensive for potential host cities. As MacAloon (2016) suggests, this has in part been motivated by a renewed public scepticism regarding the value of event bids. Just as the post-war period saw popular opinion turn against the use of public funds to support sporting mega events, recent years, particularly since the financial crash of 2008, have seen increased criticism of such lavish spending. As MacAloon (2016:767) argues: "In a nutshell, fewer and fewer global cities were interested or able to bid to host the Olympic Games. The nutmeat inside that nutshell is that Europe itself was turning against the Olympics". *Olympic Agenda 2020* (International Olympic Committee, 2014) seeks to overcome this concern, making several recommendations which centre upon the development of more sustainable bidding and delivery processes, including:

- "Introduce a new philosophy: the IOC to invite potential candidates to present an Olympic project that best matches their sports, economic and environmental long-term planning needs" (p.9).
- "The IOC to further assist Candidate Cities and reduce the cost of bidding" (p.11).
- "The IOC to take a more proactive position and leadership role with regard to sustainability and ensure it is included in all aspects of the planning and staging of the Olympic Games" (p.12).

- "The IOC to embrace sustainability principles" (p.12).
- "Reduce the cost and reinforce the flexibility of Olympic Games management" (p.15).

Similarly, *Olympic Agenda 2020* sought to address other contemporary concerns regarding sporting mega events. Although social impacts have, as argued previously, been an anticipated legacy of sporting mega events since the turn of the millennium at least, as Van Rheenen (2014) highlights, recent iterations of sporting mega events, such as the Sochi 2014 Winter Olympics, have been criticised for potential human rights violations, particularly surrounding issues of equality. In response to this, *Olympic Agenda 2020* sought to "strengthen the 6th Fundamental Principle of Olympism" (p.14) which states:

> The enjoyment of the rights and freedoms set forth in this Olympic Charter shall be secured without discrimination of any kind, such as race, colour, sex, sexual orientation, language, religion, political or other opinion, national or social origin, property, birth or other status.
>
> *(International Olympic Committee, 2015:14)*

Conclusions

This journey through the history of major event bidding demonstrates a clear trend. Just as events themselves have moved from the periphery of civic life to the centre in the last 100 years, taking on an increasingly important role in economic development, urban regeneration and global politics; so too the bidding processes surrounding major events have grown and developed to reflect this increasing importance. It is clear from the above review that the range of areas of urban renewal to which event bids must contribute has increased. From initially being expected to make no real contribution to the host city in the early 1900s, the post-war period saw the development of wider urban infrastructure emerge as a key outcome. The development agenda grew further in the 1980s with the addition of economic imperatives and the 1990s saw more and more dimensions added. In the 2000s, this process accelerated more rapidly with cultural elements, destination rebranding, environmental and social impacts being added to the requirements, almost on an event-by-event basis, as the bidding processes become ever more complex and expansive.

However, in this chapter we have also suggested that the popularity of major sporting and cultural events is cyclical. In the early 1900s, bidding processes did not even take place (Dyreson & Llewellyn, 2008), with the early iterations of what subsequently became sporting mega events (Roche, 2000) simply being 'indentured' to host cities. As the power and reputations of such events grew, so too did the number of prospective cities seeking to make use of their reach and influence. However, as costs and scale increased further, interest declined in the post-war period as cities and nations became wary of becoming the next Montreal, until by the 1980s interest in bidding had all but ceased in all corners of the globe, allowing Los Angeles to make its intervention and redirect the nature and scope of such events. Buoyed by the success of the 1984 and 1992 Games, and with the growth in power of other sporting mega events, such as the FIFA World Cup and various cultural events, the last thirty years have seen unprecedented levels of interest in hosting such events with, sometimes, dozens of nations or cities competing over single events. This cycle of popularity appears closely linked to the successful addition of a new legacy type to the perceived benefits of hosting these events. Popularity soared initially when it became clear that major events could be used to develop sporting infrastructure, before dropping as costs outweighed the benefits. The economic realignment caused by Los Angeles hosting the 1984 Olympic Games created a second boom as cities realised the opportunity to boost their economy and run major events as a profitable enterprise and Barcelona's 'model' hosting propelled this even further. As each successful bid of the 1990s and 2000s added a new dimension, so too did interest in bidding, until the high water mark of the early to mid-2000s where event bidding reached its (to date) zenith. Interestingly, the role of awarding bodies in the development of bidding processes can be identified as 'reactionary' rather than leading the agenda. As one event successfully offers a new dimension, it is thereafter incorporated into subsequent bidding processes by awarding bodies, which then force these requirements onto future hosts.

However, as the perceived rewards of hosting major events increased, so too did the risk of corruption and illegality in the bidding processes. As Chapter 7 will demonstrate in more detail, starting notably with Salt Lake City's hosting of the 2002 Winter Olympics (see Wenn & Martyn, 2006) and increasing, seemingly exponentially, into the present decade (see Pielke, 2013; Jennings 2011), major events such as the FIFA World Cups of 2010, 2018 and 2022, the Rio 2016 Olympics and the 2021 IAAF World Championships have all been tarnished by allegations of impropriety during or related to the bidding process. With allegations of bribery, corruption and criminality dogging them, the bidding processes surrounding major events are increasingly under 'reform' and will change even further in the years to come. All of this, therefore, raises interesting questions, to be considered in Chapter 11, regarding the future direction of events. What will be the emerging agendas and issues likely to face potential hosts in the years to come? What will be expected of destinations seeking access to major events? Will such events see a greater surge in popularity or do the current controversies and growing protest movements mean a period of decline will be ongoing? These issues will be examined in more detail as this book concludes, but before reaching these aspects, it is necessary to develop a more nuanced understanding of the motivations underpinning candidates' desire to bid.

References

Alegi, P. (2001) 'Feel the pull in your soul': Local agency and global trends in South Africa's 2006 World Cup Bid. *Soccer and Society*, 2(3), pp.1–21.

Andranovich, G., Burbank, M.J. and Heying, C.H. (2001) Olympic cities: Lessons learned from mega-event politics. *Journal of Urban Affairs*, 23(2), pp.113–131.

Balibrea, M.P. (2001) Urbanism, culture and the post-industrial city: Challenging the 'Barcelona model'. *Journal of Spanish Cultural Studies*, 2(2), pp.187–210.

Cantelon, H. (2000) The making of the IOC environmental policy as the third dimension of the Olympic movement. *International Review for the Sociology of Sport*, 35(3), pp.294–308.

Chalip, L. (2006) Towards social leverage of sport events. *Journal of Sport & Tourism*, 11(2), pp.109–127.

Chalkley, B. and Essex, S. (1999) Urban development through hosting international events: A history of the Olympic Games. *Planning Perspectives*, 14(4), pp.369–394.

Coaffee, J. (2013) Policy transfer, regeneration legacy and the summer Olympic Games: Lessons for London 2012 and beyond. *International Journal of Sport Policy & Politics*, 5(2), pp.295–311.

Coalter, F. (2007) London Olympics 2012: 'The catalyst that inspires people to lead more active lives'? *Perspectives in Public Health*, 127(3), p.109.

Davies, L.E. (2012) Beyond the Games: Regeneration legacies and London 2012. *Leisure Studies*, 31(3), pp.309–337.

Death, C. (2011) 'Greening' the 2010 FIFA World Cup: Environmental sustainability and the mega-event in South Africa. *Journal of Environmental Policy & Planning*, 13(2), pp.99–117.

Dolles, H. and Söderman, S. (2010) Addressing ecology and sustainability in mega-sporting events: The 2006 football World Cup in Germany. *Journal of Management & Organization*, 16(4), pp.587–600.

Dyreson, M. and Llewellyn, M. (2008) Los Angeles is the Olympic city: Legacies of the 1932 and 1984 Olympic Games. *The International Journal of the History of Sport*, 25(14), pp.1991–2018.

Essex, S. and Chalkley, B. (1998) Olympic Games: Catalyst of urban change. *Leisure Studies*, 17(3), pp.187–206.

Foley, M., McGillivray, D. and McPherson, G. (2012) *Event policy: From theory to strategy*. London: Routledge.

García, B. (2005) Deconstructing the city of culture: The long-term legacies of Glasgow 1990. *Urban Studies*, 42 (5–6), pp.841–868.

Gold, J.R. and Gold, M.M. (2008) Olympic cities: Regeneration, city rebranding and changing urban agendas. *Geography Compass*, 2(1), pp.300–318.

Gratton, C. and Preuss, H. (2008) Maximizing Olympic impacts by building up legacies. *The International Journal of the History of Sport*, 25(14), pp.1922–1938.

International Olympic Committee (IOC) (2014) *Olympic Agenda 2020: 20+20 recommendations*. Lausanne: IOC.

International Olympic Committee (2015) *Olympic Charter*. Lausanne: IOC.

Jennings, A. (2011) Investigating corruption in corporate sport: The IOC and FIFA. *International Review for the Sociology of Sport*, 46(4), pp.1–12.

Jones, P. and Wilks-Heeg, S. (2004) Capitalising culture: Liverpool 2008. *Local Economy*, 19(4), pp.341–360.

Kellett, P., Hede, A.M. and Chalip, L. (2008) Social policy for sport events: Leveraging (relationships with) teams from other nations for community benefit. *European Sport Management Quarterly*, 8(2), pp.101–121.

Kissoudi, P. (2008) The Athens Olympics: Optimistic legacies – post-Olympic assets and the struggle for their realization. *The International Journal of the History of Sport*, 25(14), pp.1972–1990.

Krüger, A. (1999) The unfinished Symphony: A history of the Olympic Games from Coubertin to Samaranch. In J. Riordan and A. Krüger (eds), *The International Politics of Sport in the Twentieth Century* (pp.3–27). London: Routledge.

Lenskyj, H.J. (2008) *Olympic industry resistance: Challenging Olympic power and propaganda.* Albany: SUNY Press.

Leopkey, B. and Parent, M.M. (2012) Olympic Games legacy: From general benefits to sustainable long-term legacy. *The International Journal of the History of Sport*, 29(6), pp.924–943.

Liao, H. and Pitts, A. (2006) A brief historical review of Olympic urbanization. *The International Journal of the History of Sport*, 23(7), pp.1232–1252.

MacAloon, J.J. (2016) Agenda 2020 and the Olympic Movement. *Sport in Society*, 19(6), pp.767–785.

Masterman, G. (2009) *Strategic sports event management.* Olympic edn. Amsterdam: Elsevier Butterworth-Heinemann.

Miah, A. and García, B. (2012) *The Olympics: The basics.* London: Routledge.

Müller, M. (2015) The mega-event syndrome: Why so much goes wrong in mega-event planning and what to do about it. *Journal of the American Planning Association*, 81(1), pp.6–17.

Nye, J.S. (2004) *Soft power: The means to success in world politics.* Cambridge, MA: PublicAffairs.

Pielke, R. (2013) How can FIFA be held accountable? *Sport Management Review*, 16(3), pp.255–267.

Richards, G. and Palmer, R. (2012) *Eventful cities.* London: Routledge.

Roche, M. (2000) *Mega-events and modernity.* London: Routledge.

Shaw, C.A. (2008) *Five rings circus: Myths and realities of the Olympic Games.* British Columbia: New Society Publishers.

Smith, A. (2012) *Events and urban regeneration: The strategic use of events to revitalise cities.* London: Routledge.

Spirou, C. (2011) *Urban tourism and urban change: Cities in a global economy.* London: Routledge.

Van Rheenen, D. (2014) A skunk at the garden party: The Sochi Olympics, state-sponsored homophobia and prospects for human rights through mega sporting events. *Journal of Sport & Tourism,* 19(2), pp.127–144.

Waitt, G. (1999) Playing games with Sydney: Marketing Sydney for the 2000 Olympics. *Urban Studies*, 36(7), pp.1055–1077.

Wenn, S.R. and Martyn, S.G. (2006) 'Tough Love': Richard Pound, David D'Alessandro, and the Salt Lake City Olympics bid scandal. *Sport in History*, 26(1), pp.64–90.

Whitson, D. and Horne, J. (2006) Part 2. The glocal politics of sports mega-events: Underestimated costs and overestimated benefits? Comparing the outcomes of sports mega-events in Canada and Japan. *The Sociological Review*, 54(s2), pp.71–89.

3

MOTIVATIONS TO BID

Introduction

In the previous chapter we examined how event bidding processes have evolved over the last 100 years as an increasing number of legacy outcomes are sought by both potential hosts and awarding bodies. Typically, these approaches focused around tangible transformations occurring within the host, as a result of winning and delivering the event in question. However, in this chapter we turn our attention to the factors underpinning and influencing the decision to bid within the prospective host destination. In addition to the standard transformations proclaimed in bid books and the campaigns surrounding the pursuit of peripatetic events, there is also a raft of hidden concepts and motivations which drive the 'will to bid'. Whilst tangible, transformative impacts typically produce standardised outputs at the delivery stage: stadia and housing developments, volunteering initiatives and skills development programmes, increased tourist flows and economic activity; the intangible factors are often unique to the locality of the individual bid. They are driven by internal motivations and host-specific socio-economic and political conditions. However, as this chapter highlights, these contextual factors are hugely influential in determining the *type* of bid produced by the specific candidate. Intangible factors permeate every aspect of the bidding process, influencing what types of event are sought in the first instance. They direct the technical construction of bids and hosting strategies, determining how the event will be delivered should success follow candidature. They influence the narrative of the bid, how it is articulated to the candidates' internal and external constituents and who must be wooed and courted as part of lobbying campaigns. These factors even influence how the bid is received and perceived by others, potentially shaping the formation of future oppositional movements. Before moving to consider each of these issues in turn in the subsequent chapters of this text, we must first understand the motivations which underpin the decision to bid. Here, we identify three core, over-arching motivations which can be seen to underpin decisions to bid: economic reframing, nation-building and place-making. It is our assertion that most stated motives within bid campaigns fall into one of these three areas. To a broad extent, these concepts are typically found underpinning most peripatetic bids in some combination and, as we demonstrate, each is contentious and requires critical consideration.

Economic reframing

As indicated in the previous chapter, major sporting and cultural event bids are often launched with the justification that they will generate profound economic transformations for the candidate if successful in winning the event (Barrios, Russell & Andrews, 2016). The nature of this transformation is typically associated with the creation of jobs directly linked to the staging and delivery of the event, the inward investment which follows from tourists flocking to it and the indirect revenues which flow as a result of undertaking such a grand project (see Stewart & Rayner, 2016). The most recent (at the time of writing) Olympic Games, Rio 2016, encapsulated this aspiration in bid documentation which claimed the event would lead to the upskilling of 48,000 adults and young people with long-term jobs for 15,000 more (Rio 2016, 2009). Similarly, Glasgow's hosting of the 2014 Commonwealth Games was reported (BBC News, 2015) to have generated £740 million for the Scottish economy and to have led to nearly 700,000 visitors travelling to the city. However, at a conceptual level the decision to bid is often indicative of a desire not just to increase economic revenues, but also to fundamentally reframe the economy of the host destination.

The use of major sporting and cultural events as a means of pursuing an economic development agenda within a locale is significant for *how* the goal is achieved as much as its actual (often-contested) attainment. Smith (2012) highlights that bidding often represents a means of highlighting that a city or state is increasingly open to working in partnership with commercial interests. As Baade & Matheson (2016) suggest, one of the primary justifications for hosting an event such as the Olympics is the desire to create a positive message about the long-term economic vitality of the host. The act of bidding becomes a declaration that a host is 'open for business' and represents a 'coming out party' (Panagiotopoulou, 2012) for the destination's brand. Foley, McGillivray & McPherson (2012) further emphasise this point with their discussion of Barcelona where former Mayor, Jordi Hereu, claimed the act of hosting the 1992 Olympics enabled the city to continue to reap inward investment well into the early twenty-first century as it retained an image of a dynamic, investment worthy economy. Toohey (2008) highlights similar claims made by Australian politicians and business people that the 2000 Sydney Games demonstrated that the nation was, not only capable of delivering a sporting mega event, but also that the country was a world class tourist destination and possessed strong financial and knowledge economies. Chalkley & Essex (1999) even highlight that failed bids such as Manchester's courting of the Olympic Games can have significant positive impacts. More recently, London's staging of the 2012 Olympic Games, as Grix & Houlihan (2014) highlight, was considered as much an opportunity to take advantage of the 'corporate networking' opportunity presented by the Games to the host nation, as it was driven by any sporting desire. A bid for a major event therefore represents an opportunity, not just to reap the benefits of that event, but also the chance to reframe the economy of the host, to infuse it with a sense of urban entrepreneurship which reaches far beyond the confines of the event and presents a new framework for working in all areas of civic life.

Boyle & Hughes (1994) examined Glasgow's reign as European Capital of Culture in 1990 and argued that the event, and subsequent bids to host other major events, enabled a symbolic reorientation of the city, whereby the city embraced a market-based approach to civic development steeped in urban entrepreneurialism. This mercantalisation becomes practically hegemonic, with all urban development viewed through a discourse which places the needs of business front and centre and as synonymous with the needs of the host. As Müller (2015a) highlights, all decisions relating to urban development become framed by the sporting mega event. As he discusses, event hosts become afflicted with 'event seizure' (Müller, 2015b), whereby: "the mega-event, and the elites associated with it, take possession of development agendas and funds and impose their own priorities" (p.2). Civic decision-making becomes infused with a neo-liberal discourse in which the language of strategic planning takes precedence over that of welfare and social good. A consumption-based landscape emerges which, as Smith (2012) highlights, enables the pursuit of new agendas and models of working which favour an increased role for business in the governance of the hosts' economy. The emergence in the last twenty years of destination marketing organisations, convention bureaus and place marketing bodies, at local and national levels, based on a mixed economy, partnership model, is indicative of this process. These bodies are forged in the spirit of urban entrepreneurship, and, in turn, through their successes, reinforce the value of such an approach, solidifying this neo-liberal economic reformation. Cities become products, and discussions of 'market share' and 'competitive advantage' enter the standard lexicon of civic life. As Spirou (2011) notes, former 'service providers' become active participants in economic affairs. In Chalip's (2006) words, civic activity such as event production can become about "economic impact rather than social value" (p.111). In the worst cases, such as Essex & Chalkley's (1998) discussion of the Atlanta Committee for the Olympic Games (ACOG), these organisations can become a form of 'privatised government'. More recently, Broudehoux & Sánchez (2016) highlight this in the context of the Rio 2016 Olympics, noting the growing role of the private sector in governance decisions through the creation of public–private partnerships. A process of 'agencification' (Grix & Houlihan, 2014), creating networks of arm's length bodies and forming public–private partnerships to drive development increases and urban development projects are pushed through as supporting the bid becomes the imperative driving civic development (see Kissoudi, 2008). Bid committees are often the thin edge of the wedge, driving this process, with Shaw (2008) highlighting their tendency to originate and operate on the margins of civic account-ability (a theme explored further in Chapter 7). The desire to compete and 'win' the rights to host a major event and to 'defeat' competitor cities and nations further fuels this process, and major events begin to represent a form of 'civic blackmail' – cities, fuelled by the deadlines of the bidding process commit to development strategies and timelines that would otherwise be scrutinised in more depth and detail.

Glasgow: transformation through events

One of the most notable cases of the use of events as a tool for economic reframing and urban transformation can be seen in Glasgow, Scotland. Indeed, Salisbury (2016), drawing on Foley et al.'s (2012) work, argues Glasgow's history can be characterised as one of reinvention. The city, Scotland's largest, has made significant use of sporting and cultural events over a thirty-year period to elicit a significant transformation of its local economy and urban and civic infrastructure. The city, which McCrone (2002) indicates styled itself as the "second city of the [British] empire" (p.14) in the early twentieth century, was at this time an industrial power-house. However, as Gomez (1998) discusses, like much of Scotland, Glasgow struggled to adjust to the rapid deindustrialisation which followed the Second World War. By the 1970s, Glasgow was characterised as a:

> filthy, slum-ridden, poverty-stricken, gang-infested city whose population consisted of undersized, incomprehensible, drunken, foul-mouthed, sectarian lumpen proletarians who were prone to hit each other with broken bottles and razors without warning.
>
> *(Damer, 1990:5)*

This negative image and reputation, combined with the economic stagnation and mass unemployment, meant that the city required significant state and market inter-vention and redevelopment. This process was kickstarted, as Smith (2012) highlights, by the decision of the then Lord Provost, Michael Kelly, to successfully pursue the title of 1990 European Capital of Culture. The bid saw Glasgow become the first city to use the European Capital of Culture title as a catalyst to accelerate urban regeneration (Mittag, 2013). Whilst García (2004) suggests the city could have done more to capitalise on the legacy opportunities of 1990, Glasgow, in the years pre-ceding and following its reign as European Capital of Culture, it developed a strong track record of hosting major events, both hallmark and peripatetic (Richards & Palmer, 2012). From the Garden Festival (1988) to the UK City of Architecture and Design (1999), to the UEFA Champions League Final (2003), and culminating with the 2014 Commonwealth Games, Glasgow has gained a reputation as a successful event host and, as Higham & Hinch (2009) highlight, has changed from a city in decline to one appearing vibrant and healthy.

However, this remaking of the city image can also be seen to have more than simply a brand identity impact. In addition to his image of filthy slums, Damer

(1990) argued that in the eyes of some, "to make matters worse, Glaswegians were infected with the Red peril; Glasgow was a robustly socialist city" (p.5). As such, the transformation of the city into a destination city also offered an opportunity to reframe the city as a neo-liberal economic powerhouse. As Glasgow's event-led regeneration gathered pace, it was telling that the city council lauded "the transformation of Glasgow from its inward-looking, post-industrial slump to a confident, outward-looking, economically regenerated destination city" (Bhandari, 2014:50).

Mooney's (2004) critique of Glasgow's turn as European Capital of Culture and the events which followed notes how the 'new' Glasgow, a city of enterprise and creativity, was constructed directly against the 'old' Glasgow of statist intervention, and he cites McLay's remark that: "the Year of Culture has more to do with power politics than culture" (Mooney, 2004:331). Whilst Glasgow's transformation over the last thirty years can be understood as a seminal exercise in place rebranding, it must also be understood as a significant economic and political reframing of the city and the focus of its urban renewal.

Nation building

Major events have a long track record of being used as a facet of nation-building projects. Miah & García (2012) are among the many to have investigated, for example, the role of the 1936 Olympics, which gave the Olympic movement much of its current symbolism, in developing a sense of German nationhood in keeping with Nazi values in the lead up to the Second World War. Such efforts, as Cornelissen (2008) highlights, take advantage of the social momentum and emotional tide of sporting mega events to buttress the desired nation-building project, securing consent with a mass media spectacle promoting the desired expression of nationalism and patriotism. However, increasingly even the bidding stage for major events can be seen as playing a role in nation building. For many cities and nations, a key motivation underpinning their bidding for a major event is the ability to use this event as a means of creating and articulating a particular notion of place to those residing within. Kersting (2007) notes Germany's use of the 2006 FIFA World Cup as a means of enabling an articulation of German national identity, free from the stigma of the Second World War, whilst Smith (2012) highlights South Africa's use of the following FIFA World Cup as means of strengthening its fledgling, post-Apartheid democracy, with the bid documentation (South Africa 2010, 2004) even directly referencing "a people who struggled for and won their liberation, dignity and democracy" (p.11). Xu (2006) highlights the importance of the Beijing Olympics in 2008 in articulating China's position as a world power externally, but also, importantly, for convincing the Chinese population itself, via the 'New Beijing, Great Olympics' objective, of the strength of the state's new vision of a 'harmonious socialist society'.

Commenting on the last three Olympic bid cycles, Cha (2016:139) highlights the power ascribed to sporting mega events:

When Vladimir Putin won the bid for the 2014 Sochi Games, he proclaimed that "Russia is back." When Beijing hosted the 2008 Olympics, they portrayed the Games as marking three decades of Chinese modernization dating back to Deng Xiaoping. Prime Minister Shinzo Abe (2014) celebrated Tokyo's winning the bid later by calling it a "major catalyst through which Japan will be born anew." These and many other examples show that mega sporting events like the Olympics become benchmarks for a nation.

Tellingly, upon becoming Scotland's First Minister, Alex Salmond, then Leader of the pro-independence Scottish Nationalist Party, pledged to continue supporting Glasgow's 2014 Commonwealth Games bid, initiated under a New Labour government, on the basis that the Commonwealth Games were one of the few athletics events in which Scotland competes as an *independent* nation. The bid, and subsequent hosting of the event, represented an opportunity for a discreet but significant articulation of Scottish national identity over a number of years, culminating with the eventual hosting of the Games in the summer of 2014, which themselves took place just weeks before a referendum on Scottish independence.

Understanding event bids as a means of constructing a shared identity therefore makes it easier to understand why so many emerging nations, for whom the development of such a coherent identity is often a priority, have joined the event bidding circuit in recent years. Nations attempting to shake off their historic geopolitical identities, such as ex-Soviet states or post-Apartheid or civil-war scarred African nations, can make use of such bids to articulate and consolidate a new national identity. Using David Black's (2007) term, there is need to understand "The Symbolic Politics of Sport Mega-events". Bidding for such sporting mega events, whilst undoubtedly linked to the search for the forms of impact outlined in the previous chapter, can increasingly be understood as a symbolic expression of statehood, albeit a contested one. Whilst major sporting and cultural event bids allow an articulation of a national identity, it is worth asking *what* national identity is expressed through the bid and *whose* interests are served by the chosen expression. Grix & Houlihan (2014) highlight the intention of London to use its 2012 Olympic bid to promote and reinforce values of "tolerance, moderation and openness" (p.585); values which would seemingly be beyond reproach. However, it is worth noting that such values were linked to the enhancement of national security, suggesting a nation-building agenda which specifically targeted those within the society who may be perceived to possess alternative views which are seen as a threat to such security. However, if transposed into other settings, for example communist or totalitarian states or those where the articulation of a homogenous, 'native' cultural identity is less clear cut, the conflation of nation building and national security raises questions regarding the promotion of a dominant identity over others who may wish to contest such expression. In this context, Xu's (2006) aforementioned discussion of China's use of the Beijing 2008 Olympics to express and reinforce a "harmonious socialist society" (p.97) feels more problematic. With the increasing number of bids originating in nations outside the Western liberal democratic states which have previously dominated peripatetic event bidding and hosting cycles, this notion is increasingly worthy of study, particularly with Foley et al. (2012) arguing that there may even be advantages in the bidding process to being a non-democratic state.

Global positioning

In addition to renegotiating the relationship between destination and indigenous population, the decision to bid for a major event can also be driven by a desire to renegotiate the relationship between the host and external audiences. Increasingly, as Chapter 6 will show in more detail, national governments view the hosting of major sporting and cultural events as part of their cultural diplomacy arsenal, granting them position and status on the world stage (Grix & Houlihan, 2014). Previously, it has been highlighted that the move towards an entrepreneurial city has been indicative of being 'open for business'; this notion drives many event bids, typically attached by an attempt to remake the image of the host in the eyes of the outside world, and, subsequently, render a new impression through the successful hosting of the event (Andranovich, Burbank & Heying, 2001). Such attempts to engage in what Smith (2005) refers to as "re-imaging" (p.399) enables hosts to accrue economic, cultural and political capital through the (re)presentation and (re)production of their image. Kissoudi (2008) highlights this clearly by discussing Greece's hosting of the 2004 Olympics as affording the nation the opportunity to reposition itself on the world stage as a modern metropolis, more than simply a collection of ancient architecture and historic sites. Grix & Houlihan (2014) assert similar motivations as underpinning Delhi's bid for the 2010 Commonwealth Games as well as Brazil's 2014 FIFA World Cup and 2016 Olympic bids and Qatar's decision to bid for the FIFA World Cup. Similar motives could be ascribed to Baku's (Azerbaijan) bid for the inaugural European Games in 2015 and the failed Almaty (Kazakhstan) bid for the 2022 Winter Olympics. In each case, a developing or emerging nation attempts to (re)position itself on the world stage by securing the right to host a sporting mega event.

This repositioning can have serious repercussions beyond the boundaries of the bidding nation, causing a renegotiation of relationships between the prospective host and its neighbours. Cornelissen (2008), for example, highlights how South Africa used its bids for both the 2006 and 2010 FIFA World Cups as a means of not only announcing its arrival on the world stage, but also asserting a position of leadership, even dominance, in the wider African continent in terms of relationships with the rest of the world and the articulation of an 'African' identity. Similarly, Brannagan & Giulianotti (2015) examine the power of Qatar's 2022 bid in renegotiating the Gulf state's relationship within the region and the outside world, positioning the previously unheralded nation at the centre of the region and raising its global standing. Indeed, as Cornelissen (2008) highlights, major events are one of the most powerful tools available to these developing nations in gaining a seat of prominence at the world table, as the 'soft power' (Nye, 2004) accrued for hosting such events is more readily available to such nations than the economic or military might required to exercise harder forms of status and prestige.

In each case, it is the attempted 'purchase' of a major event, in the hope of brand transference to the host which acts as the catalyst to the (re)positioning effort. Previously 'unknown' nations and cities attempt to kickstart their destination branding campaign with the acquisition of an event with an already clearly recognised identity in the hope it will drive attention towards their offering. Other, 'established', nations hope that association with a higher order event brand will bring about a step change in their destination awareness, and move them into the next tier of global cities. Shoval (2002) suggests that tier one, alpha cities view winning the right to host the biggest events as a means of staying ahead of the chasing pack. Interestingly, Masterman's (2009) work suggests that in the case of some bids, such as the Winter Olympic bids of Salt Lake City (for 2002) and Torino (2006), such strategies are not even dependent on winning hosting rights, although both did. Rather simple association, through what Brighenti et al. (2005) term 'alibi bids', with the bidding process is sufficient to achieve the requisite development effect. Whilst Fourie & Santana-Gallego (2011) suggest the return on investment is smaller than for winning bids, they agree that there is a positive return for simply taking part in the bidding process. Shoval's (2002) work takes this one step further, implying that, for smaller destinations, there is potentially more to be gained from association via bidding than winning the right to host, with all of the problematic issues this incurs. Regardless of how eager a nation may be to actually win hosting rights, it is the notion that bidding accrues place brand awareness that underpins these strategies. Cities and nations are able to complement their "aspirational destination brand" (Foley et al., 2012:82) through association with an appropriate, related peripatetic event, tying their brand story to the requirements and scope of the event. Bids for sporting events emphasise the sporting prowess and history of the city and its residents; cultural events see a focus on the heritage and history of the place in an attempt to entwine place with event and convince tourists, investors and the outside world of the personality of the destination brand.

However, such positioning campaigns are not as straightforward as they might seem. Firstly, as Smith (2012) highlights, hitching a destination brand to that of a major event may actually restrict the possibility of forcing a wholesale change of the overall destination brand, as the place becomes secondary to the more prominent and powerful brand of the event itself, something Müller (2015a) identifies as a key symptom of 'mega-event syndrome'. Where they are successful, Foley et al. (2012) and Spirou (2011) raise questions about how the host is portrayed in such re-imaginations of place and who benefits from the redevelopment, with the former highlighting the emphasis on 'elite and folkloric' interpretations of the host, and the latter suggesting it leads to the creation of two tier cities, where the wealthy middle class are represented and the poor pushed to the periphery in economic, physical and cultural terms. Beyond this, Grix & Houlihan (2014) raise questions regarding the 'soft power' dimensions of bidding, highlighting that there is no clear pathway between hosting a major event and transforming the supposedly accrued power into a concrete benefit to the host. Even more critically, they highlight the damage done to the reputations of nations or cities, such as Athens or Delhi, when a major event is perceived to be poorly hosted, resulting in 'soft disempowerment', a theme examined in more detail in Chapter 6. Such situations reduce the impact of a successful bid and render future bids less likely to succeed.

Conclusions

Major event bids are deeply politicised activities, clearly motivated by a desire to pursue a range of agendas. Increasingly, they are used as a tool not just for transformation of the host in an overtly noticeable manner, as indicated in Chapter 2, but also to create a culture change at a subconscious level. Cities and nations are remade through bidding processes, infused with new guiding principles, values and ideals. These processes, as this chapter demonstrates, are not without contestation and the new ethos embedded into hosts is not value neutral. Increasingly, bids have come to embed a new urban entrepreneurialism into the practice, indeed psyche, of urban development. The values of dominant groups are increasingly expressed through bid campaigns and are reinforced and reiterated as the values of the host moving forward. This, as will be shown in the coming chapters, is then identifiable within the structure and narrative of the bids such prospective hosts produce, and reinforced yet further through their successes.

References

Andranovich, G., Burbank, M.J. and Heying, C.H. (2001) Olympic cities: Lessons learned from mega-event politics. *Journal of Urban Affairs*, 23(2), pp.113–131.

Baade, R.A. and Matheson, V.A. (2016) Going for the gold: The economics of the Olympics. *The Journal of Economic Perspectives*, 30(2), pp.201–218.

Barrios, D., Russell, S. and Andrews, M. (2016) *Bringing home the gold? A review of the economic impact of hosting mega-events* (No. 320). Center for International Development at Harvard University.

BBC News. (2015) Glasgow 2014 Commonwealth Games 'worth £740m to economy'. Available at http://www.bbc.co.uk/news/uk-scotland-glasgow-west-33626350 (accessed 15 March 2017).

Bhandari, K. (2014) *Tourism and national identity: Heritage and nationhood in Scotland* (Vol. 39). Clevedon: Channel View Publications.

Black, D. (2007) The symbolic politics of sport mega-events: 2010 in comparative perspective. *Politikon*, 34(3), pp.261–276.

Boyle, M. and Hughes, G. (1994) The politics of urban entrepreneurialism in Glasgow. *Geoforum*, 25(4), pp.453–470.

Brannagan, P.M. and Giulianotti, R. (2015) Soft power and soft disempowerment: Qatar, global sport and football's 2022 World Cup finals. *Leisure Studies*, 34(6), pp.703–719.

Brighenti, O., Clivaz, C., Délétroz, N. and Favre, N. (2005) *From initial idea to success: A guide to bidding for sports events for politicians and administrators.* Chavannes-Lausanne, Switzerland: Sports Event Network for Tourism and Economic Development of the Alpine Space.

Broudehoux, A-M. and Sánchez, F. (2016) The politics of mega-event planning in Rio de Janeiro: Contesting the Olympic city of exception. In V. Viehoff and G. Poynter (eds), *Mega-event Cities: Urban legacies of global sports events* (pp.109–122). London: Routledge

Cha, V. (2016) Role of sport in international relations: National rebirth and renewal. *Asian Economic Policy Review*, 11(1), pp.139–155.

Chalip, L. (2006) Towards social leverage of sport events. *Journal of Sport & Tourism*, 11(2), pp.109–127.

Chalkley, B. and Essex, S. (1999) Urban development through hosting international events: A history of the Olympic Games. *Planning Perspectives*, 14(4), pp.369–394.

Cornelissen, S. (2008) Scripting the nation: Sport, mega-events, foreign policy and state-building in post-apartheid South Africa 1. *Sport in Society*, 11(4), pp.481–493.

Damer, S. (1990) *Glasgow: Going for a song*. London: Lawrence & Wishart.

Essex, S. and Chalkley, B. (1998) Olympic Games: Catalyst of urban change. *Leisure Studies*, 17(3), pp.187–206.

Foley, M., McGillivray, D. and McPherson, G. (2012) *Event policy: From theory to strategy*. London: Routledge.

Fourie, J. and Santana-Gallego, M. (2011) The impact of mega-sport events on tourist arrivals. *Tourism Management*, 32(6), pp.1364–1370.

García, B. (2004) Urban regeneration, arts programming and major events: Glasgow 1990, Sydney 2000 and Barcelona 2004. *International Journal of Cultural Policy*, 10(1), pp.103–118.

Gomez, M.V. (1998) Reflective images: The case of urban regeneration in Glasgow and Bilbao. *International Journal of Urban & Regional Research*, 22(1), pp.106–121.

Grix, J. and Houlihan, B. (2014) Sports mega-events as part of a nation's soft power strategy: The cases of Germany (2006) and the UK (2012). *The British Journal of Politics & International Relations*, 16(4), pp.572–596.

Higham, J. and Hinch, T. (2009) *Sport and tourism: Globalization, mobility and identity*. London: Routledge.

Kersting, N. (2007) Sport and national identity: A Comparison of the 2006 and 2010 FIFA World Cups™. *Politikon*, 34(3), pp.277–293.

Kissoudi, P. (2008) The Athens Olympics: Optimistic legacies – post-Olympic assets and the struggle for their realization. *The International Journal of the History of Sport*, 25(14), pp.1972–1990.

Masterman, G. (2009) *Strategic sports event management*. Olympic edn. Amsterdam: Elsevier Butterworth-Heinemann.

McCrone, D. (2002) *Understanding Scotland: The sociology of a nation*. London: Routledge.

Miah, A. and García, B. (2012) *The Olympics: The basics*. London: Routledge.

Mittag, J. (2013) The changing concept of the European Capitals of Culture: Between the endorsement of European identity and city advertising. In K. Patel (ed.), *The cultural politics of Europe: European Capitals of Culture and European Union since the 1980s* (pp.39–54). Routledge: London.

Mooney, G. (2004) Cultural policy as urban transformation? Critical reflections on Glasgow, European City of Culture 1990. *Local Economy*, 19(4), pp.327–340.

Müller, M. (2015a) The mega-event syndrome: Why so much goes wrong in mega-event planning and what to do about it. *Journal of the American Planning Association*, 81(1), pp.6–17.

Müller, M. (2015b): How mega-events capture their hosts: Event seizure and the World Cup 2018 in Russia, *Urban Geography*. doi:10.1080/02723638.2015.1109951.

Nye, J.S. (2004) *Soft power: The means to success in world politics*. Cambridge, MA: Public Affairs.

Panagiotopoulou, R. (2012) Nation branding and the Olympic Games: New media images for Greece and China. *The International Journal of the History of Sport*, 29(16), pp.2337–2348.

Richards, G. and Palmer, R. (2012) *Eventful cities*. London: Routledge.

Rio 2016 (2009) *Rio 2016 candidature file*. Rio 2016.

Salisbury, P. (2016) An analysis of Glasgow's decision to bid for the 2014 Commonwealth Games. *Sport in Society*. doi:10.1080/17430437.2017.1232365.

Shaw, C.A. (2008) *Five ring circus: Myths and realities of the Olympic Games*. British Columbia: New Society Publishers.

Shoval, N. (2002) A new phase in the competition for the Olympic gold: The London and New York bids for the 2012 Games. *Journal of Urban Affairs*, 24(5), pp.583–599.

Smith, A. (2005) Conceptualizing city image change: The 're-imaging' of Barcelona. *Tourism Geographies*, 7(4), pp.398–423.

Smith, A. (2012) *Events and urban regeneration: The strategic use of events to revitalise cities*. London: Routledge.

South Africa 2010 (2004) *South Africa 2010 Bid Book*, South Africa 2010.

Spirou, C. (2011) *Urban tourism and urban change: Cities in a global economy*. London: Routledge.

Stewart, A. and Rayner, S. (2016) Planning mega-event legacies: Uncomfortable knowledge for host cities. *Planning Perspectives*, 31(2), pp.157–179.

Toohey, K. (2008) The Sydney Olympics: Striving for legacies – overcoming short-term disappointments and long-term deficiencies. *The International Journal of the History of Sport*, 25(14), pp.1953–1971.

Xu, X. (2006) Modernizing China in the Olympic spotlight: China's national identity and the 2008 Beijing Olympiad. *The Sociological Review*, 54(s2), pp.90–107.

PART II

Persuasion: competencies and campaigns

4

BIDDING INFRASTRUCTURE

Demonstrating technical competency

Introduction

The development of a successful event bid is an exceptionally complex process. Demonstrating to an awarding body that a candidate is capable of hosting a major event requires considerable expertise across a wide range of areas. Typically, this expertise is demonstrated via a 'bid book' or 'candidate file' which lays out in detail the technical, economic, political and legal elements, among others, of the bid and articulates the candidate's plan to operationalise the core event concept. In one of the few texts to actually examine the technicality of this process, Masterman (2009) suggests that producing bid books is a massive undertaking, running to multiple volumes and covering a range of themes and issues relevant to the delivery of the event. In the context of the 2016 Summer Olympic Games, for example, the IOC Candidate Questionnaire (International Olympic Committee (IOC), 2008) designated seventeen separate thematic areas which required a response within the bid book, with the supporting instructions running to several hundred pages. These bid books are normally prepared by a bid committee, formed from a wide range of stakeholders to demonstrate the 'technical competency' of the potential host. In the case of sporting mega-events they are also supplemented by inspection visits from the awarding body to review the capability of the candidate first-hand. These visits are carefully choreographed by the candidate to maximise success and showcase the prospective host at its finest (see Chapter 7 for more detail). This chapter examines how prospective hosts demonstrate technical competency during the bidding process. It begins by exploring how bid committees are formed, who the key stakeholders are and what they bring to the bidding process, as well as offering an analysis of the various individuals and groups included in these committees. The chapter critiques the motives of these groups and their relationships to one another, as well as the implications for the prospective host in bringing them together. The chapter also examines the process of developing the bid book itself, considering various components required in order to successfully secure hosting rights. Finally, the chapter turns its attention to the evaluation of bids by awarding bodies, examining the process and technical criteria which guide them when making a decision regarding the most technically capable prospective host.

Building bid committees

In his analysis of the aborted Boston 2024 Olympic bid, Lauermann (2016) argues that to bid, "is to enrol in multiple networks of professionalized expertise" (p.2). Despite the enormous power and influence they subsequently wield over the bidding process, the formation of bidding teams for major events receives little formal attention in the academic or grey literature. This may be due in part to the public lifecycle of bids. As Theodoraki (2007) highlights, by the time a bid intention is announced to the world, a working group comprising the beginnings of a bid team must already exist in order to have formulated this announcement. However, this also means that the formulation of bidding teams often occurs without significant public scrutiny. In recent years, particularly at the level of sporting mega events, a light has been shone on these processes, mainly through the work of those engaged in anti-bid, anti-event protest movements (see Lenskyj, 2008; Shaw, 2008). In each case, it is significant to note that the actual delivery of the bid is almost always driven by a bid committee. Which is at least overseen by a national or municipal public sector organisation. In contrast, the initial idea to bid can be traced to a small number of private individuals, typically local entrepreneurs and owners of commercial organisations. Griffiths (2000) traces the failed Cape Town 2004 and South Africa 2006 Olympic and FIFA World Cup bids to Raymond Ackerman and Irvin Khoza, respectively. Shaw (2008) locates the original catalyst for Vancouver's 2010 Winter Olympics as residing with Jack Poole. In each incidence, these were wealthy businessmen with significant personal fortunes and strong political connections and influence. These individuals, best understood as 'boosters' (see Hiller, 2000; Whitson & Horne, 2006) promote the benefits of a bid behind the scenes. They often, as Lenskyj (2008) highlights in her discussion of Daniel Doctoroff's involvement with New York's failed bid for the 2012 Olympics, reap massive benefits from the capital investment opportunities linked to major events. The behind the scenes use of political connection and power have led some to question the extent to which bid developments act only as a legitimation for business interests (Hiller, 2000), a theme which will be examined in more detail in Chapter 7.

As Theodoraki (2007) highlights, from this initial spark, bid committees typically follow a similar development pattern as they progress through the bidding process, growing and drawing in greater numbers of members and associates as the bid reaches fruition. This is intended to demonstrate the experience and knowledge possessed by the candidate (Westerbeek, Turner & Ingerson, 2002) and reassure awarding bodies of their capability to deliver. Regardless of their origin, bid committees contain several archetypal characters from the host community. These figures can best be understood through a variation of Richards & Palmer's (2010) discussion of stakeholder networks and the notion of stakeholder salience. In their text, Richards & Palmer (2010) highlight how an 'eventful city' must balance the needs of a variety of stakeholders who will possess differing levels of influence over the development of a cultural programme or strategy within a locale. Each stakeholder, building on Mitchell, Agle & Wood's (1997) notion of stakeholder salience, can be understood to possess, to some extent, one of three attributes: *power, legitimacy* and *urgency*. When examining bid committees, the intention is to bring in individuals or representatives of agencies who contribute one or more of these elements into the committee. Theodoraki (2007) highlights that bid committees will often bring together prominent politicians at local and national levels, local delivery agencies and representatives of destination marketing bodies. These representatives provide *legitimacy* to the bid committee as elected representatives, civil servants and 'official' voices of the people which is rarely questioned (Richards & Palmer, 2012). Similarly, prominent academics and academic institutions are often brought into the fold to provide intellectual legitimacy to projects. This can be in the form of long-term research projects such as Liverpool's 2008 European Capital of Culture's 'Impacts '08', which saw two local institutions delivering long-term evaluation of the impact and legacy of the year-long programme. Alternatively, or additionally, this can be in the form of educational partnerships linked to skills development and professional qualification, such as the relationship between the Gold Coast 2018 Commonwealth Games and Griffiths University in Australia. Indeed, a review of almost any major event bid will see that higher and further education institutions are typically amongst the first partners announced.

The influence and power of prominent local businesses, through organisations such as Chambers of Commerce or Business Improvement Districts are typically sought. Figures from the business community provide further legitimacy, in this case strengthening the economic case for a bid. Additionally, through providing access to the commercial sector and being able to speak 'the language of business', they also have the *power* to unlock further investment and buy in within the local environment. Similarly, depending on the nature of the event, related professional figures of repute are brought into the bid committee in key roles in order to leverage access and provide an element of control over the professional community. Most prominently, the appointment of Sebastian Coe to the role of Chair of London's 2012 Olympic bid demonstrates this process. As a prominent Olympian, Coe not only acted as a legitimate voice for the bid, but was also able to use his political connections, both in the sporting sector and the wider UK political system, to gain wider buy in for London's bid. A more local, but interesting, example can be identified in comparing the Bid Directors appointed by Aberdeen and Paisley, Scotland, for the UK City of Culture title in 2017 and 2021, respectively. Aberdeen, seeking to influence the business community in the city to play a larger role in the arts, appointed a key figure within the city's economic development forum to this role, reasoning that she would be able to talk to business and use her influence to open up opportunities. In contrast, Paisley, seeking to demonstrate that the city did indeed have a strong cultural foundation on which to base a bid, appointed a key figure from the local arts sector in order to exert influence over this element of the local economy.

Bid committees also frequently bring prominent celebrity figures or 'ambassadors' into the fold in more informal roles. David Beckham's role on behalf of London's 2012 Olympic bid is perhaps the standard bearer for this approach, which positioned him as a local hero campaigning to bring the Games to the East End of the city in which he grew up. However, similar strategies have made use of external figures as key ambassadors such as Qatar's 2022 FIFA World Cup bid, which employed famous French footballer Zinedine Zidane as a key spokesperson and supporter of their bid. Returning to Richards & Palmer's (2010) discussion of power, legitimacy and urgency, these appointments can be best understood as a variation on the *urgency* element. In their work, Richards & Palmer (2010) define urgency as "the extent to which stakeholders can make a claim on immediate attention" (p.150). In their context this reflects a claim made on the attention of the event organisers. Here, we suggest urgency can be understood as the extent to which these ambassadorial figures can promote the message of the bid committee to the wider world and convince them of the merits of the bid. Rather than a press release from a civil servant or unknown figure from the business world, a photo opportunity and press conference with a global celebrity will carry the message of the bid team further and faster and be received much more willingly by the general public, in addition to providing positive brand association with the appropriate figure. This use of celebrity is unpacked further in Chapter 7. Bid committees are also supplemented by a sub-level of experienced professional elites and civil servant figures who have the subject knowledge and expertise to produce the actual bid documentation, strategic programming and manage the capital projects required to operationalise the bid.

However, the formation of these bid committees raises a range of interesting questions and issues. Firstly, questions can be raised regarding who is considered to be a legitimate or powerful voice to be appointed to a bid committee. The landscapes of sporting and cultural economies within any city or nation are complicated and fragmented, with multiple stakeholders, associations and bodies often claiming the authority to represent their sector. This raises the question of which organisations are invited into the inner sanctum of the bid team, as there is a mutual reinforcement of value associated to being a member of a bid committee. The committee is strengthened by having a voice, but that voice is also elevated above all others in return. It is important to consider the representativeness of committees, including whether particular forms of activity are prioritised over others, leaving some groups marginalised and their activities ignored. As discussed previously, a great deal of cultural programming focuses on elite expressions of culture and identity over more inclusive forms (Foley, McGillivray & McPherson, 2012). When the representatives of these cultural forms are appointed to bid committees over others, it raises the risk of a lack of representation at best, or the possibility of being discriminatory at worst.

Secondly, the formation of large bid committees which draw from various areas of expertise and knowledge could be seen as having the effect of stifling debate surrounding the validity and value of an event bid at an early stage in the development process. By drawing in stakeholders, such as academics, early in the process, establishing them as part of the solution and creating collective responsibility for the delivery of the bid, it is far less likely that such individuals or organisations will be in a position to offer a neutral critique of the bid concept. Similarly, encouraging political figures to link their personal capital to the success of the project early in the process ensures promotion rather than probity. Whether this is a deliberate attempt to create a near hegemonic position of support for the bid, or an unintended consequence of attempts to build a broad coalition to maximise the possibility of success, there is a danger that bids are not scrutinised in enough detail prior to the point of no return, when a bid is announced and expense and energy must be allocated to seeing the project through. This theme is explored further in Chapters 6, 7 and 8.

Thirdly, as Theodoraki (2007) highlights, bid committees are eager to demonstrate the strength of their bid through the creation of a strong committee, one which can demonstrate the all important capacity and capability to deliver the eventual event successfully. This has led in recent years to a global circuit of 'bid gurus' who move from city to city and nation to nation offering their expertise, knowledge and connections to prospective hosts. Liverpool's 2008 European Capital of Culture bid drew upon the expertise of the Chairman of Manchester's bids for the 1996 and 2000 Olympics and 2002 Commonwealth Games. Aberdeen's failed bid to be UK City of Culture in 2017 made significant note of having appointed a key figure from Pafos' bid to be 2017 European Capital of Culture, who subsequently played an important role in Kalamata's 2021 European Capital of Culture bid. This peripatetic workforce, which moves on immediately following the conclusion of a bid, challenges notions inherent in many bids of developing internal capacity and achieving a legacy of cultural sustainability within the host. In addition, as practitioners move from candidate to candidate, the risk of 'by the numbers bids' increases. In a manner similar to how successful cultural regeneration projects are copied with a view to, for example, 'doing a Glasgow' (Mooney, 2004) or following the 'Barcelona model' (Balibrea, 2001), candidate cities and nations may be tempted to hire a 'bid guru' with a view to replicating a successful bid from elsewhere in the world. This leads to a formulaic approach to bidding, which focusses less on the unique history and assets of the candidate, or the local problems and issues requiring attention, and more on following a well-worn path focussed around a few key principles. Ironically, given its status as role model to many other cities seeking to follow its example, Glasgow through its city marketing bureau, and Scotland in general through its national agency, EventScotland, have offered an alternative to this in recent years; establishing bodies and forums with a specific bidding remit and focus upon the development of an institutional memory within the destination as a means to ensuring a strategic approach to bidding which spans a range of events across a range of sectors.

Aberdeen 2017: constructing a team

The construction of bid committees which meet all of these criteria is best outlined by looking at the specific case of Aberdeen's unsuccessful bid to be the 2017 UK City of Culture. Aberdeen launched this bid in the summer of 2012, formally submitting its documentation in February the following year. The city was one of eleven towns and cities vying for the title, awarded in November 2017 to the English city Hull by a panel of experts appointed by the UK Government's Department for Culture, Media and Sport (DCMS). Aberdeen's attempt to win the UK City of Culture title was articulated in its thirty-page bid document entitled *Illuminating the North* (Aberdeen 2017, 2013), which detailed the city's artistic vision for the event as well as the technical aspects of its delivery including its funding package and the city's operational experience.

The document was the product of the 'bid team' appointed by the City Council but operating at arm's length with its own independence and scope. The team was comprised of four key figures considered by the Council to possess the relevant technical expertise required to deliver such a complex project. The bid was led by a Bid Manager who had previously held a prominent role within the Aberdeen City and Shire Economic Future (ACSEF) group. Her experience delivering large-scale projects in the city was considered to give her both credibility as a leader and the connections required across the city's business community to successfully manage the bid. In addition, the city appointed an event bidding expert from Greece who was brought to the city, having worked as Executive Manager for Pafos' 2017 European Capital of Culture bid, in the role of Bid Coordinator to provide the cultural programming expertise required for the bid documentation. These key figures were joined by a professional fundraiser in the role of Funding and International Officer and an experienced press officer who acted as Marketing and Communications Officer for the bid, both of whom were heralded for their significant experience in related fields. This team of four comprised the core leadership group for the bid process, and between them they were intended to provide the *legitimacy* to assure the DCMS awarding panel that the city had the requisite experience to deliver the UK City of Culture award if successful.

The bid team was overseen by the City Council's 'UK City of Culture Sub-Committee' which was charged with the responsibility of providing a robust framework of governance and reporting for the bid. This committee served to provide both further legitimacy for the bid and to ensure the city's *powerful* figures were represented either through direct membership or invited consultant roles. The committee drew upon elected officials from each of the major parties within the City Council and included all three of the city's further and higher education institutions. It made use of the city's cultural community, with bodies such as Aberdeen Performing Arts represented and prominent figures from local arts festivals invited to contribute. The city's business community was represented through agencies such as the aforementioned ACSEF and the Aberdeen and Grampian Chamber of Commerce, ensuring commercial perspectives were enshrined in the heart of the bid. Finally, representatives of the local media were engaged with the Committee through local publisher Aberdeen Journals.

The output of the bid team was communicated via a long line of local and Scottish celebrities such as musician Emeli Sande, percussionist Dame Evelyn Glennie, prominent author Stuart McBride and comedian Billy Connolly. These figures were often used as ambassadors for the bid, making public appearances and proclamations at key points in the bid process, using the *urgency* their fame afforded to ensure maximum reach for the bid's messages and stories.

However, despite the careful construction of this team, Aberdeen's bid to be UK City of Culture fell short at the first shortlisting stage, being eliminated at this point alongside bids from Chester, East Kent, Hastings and Bexhill on Sea, Plymouth, Southend-on-Sea and a joint bid from Portsmouth and Southampton, whilst Dundee, Leicester and Swansea Bay saw their bids taken through to the final shortlist alongside the eventual winner, Hull.

Bid documents

Once the bid committee is established, the formal process of bidding for the event can begin in earnest. As each event varies in terms of the size and shape of its bidding process, it is not possible to outline a one size fits all pathway to delivering a bid. Indeed, given the issues raised in the previous section, such reductionism would not be desirable even if it were possible. However, it is possible to identify a series of issues which are common to all bids, whether this be the multi-year, multi-million pound campaigns for a sporting mega event or the significantly smaller, less expensive campaigns which surround events such as UK City of Culture awards. These issues typically find expression in the candidate file submitted by the prospective host and include a statement of motivation, evidence of political support, compliance with the technical and legal requirements of the awarding body, evidence of financial capacity, an outline of physical infrastructure and a demonstration of more intangible aspects related to experience of hosting such events.

The statement of motivation, defined by the IOC as the 'compass' which aligns all elements of the bid (International Olympic Committee, 2013), outlines the vision of the prospective host. This is an opportunity for the candidate to explain why they are bidding and, in terms of the UK City of Culture bid guidelines (Department for Culture, Media and Sport (DCMS), 2013), what is unique about the prospective bid. This is intended to demonstrate that there is a clear understanding of how the event could be used within the host for maximum effect. It is also, as the following chapter demonstrates, an opportunity for the host to develop a 'narrative' to guide their bid.

Evidence of political support takes the form of testimonial letters from relevant heads of state and political leaders at the local and national levels (Masterman, 2009). These testimonials, particularly when written by elected officials, demonstrate the implied support of the wider civic population within the prospective host for the event bid. However, they also formalise the relationship between the candidate city/nation and the awarding body, symbolically cementing the notion that the host is formally committed to delivering the promises made by the bid committee within the pages of the document.

Political support is reinforced with a series of technical and legal guarantees from the host to the awarding body committing the candidate city to delivering the terms of the bid book and enshrining the demands of the awarding body into the practices of the prospective host. In the context of the IOC and the bidding process for the 2022 Winter Olympics, this process included no less than ten separate letters of guarantee across areas such as accommodation, anti-doping processes, access to communication tools, immigration and travel and trademark protection, with a broad guarantee that any candidate would uphold the Olympic Charter:

> Names of duly authorised representatives hereby confirm that the name of the host country's NOC and name of the city authorities will respect and comply with all obligations set out in the Olympic Charter.
>
> *(IOC, 2013:83)*

The 2018 Commonwealth Games bid criteria contained nearly fifty such guarantee requests and required involvement from groups including venue owners and candidate city authorities up to national governments. These guarantees are typically expressed in complex legalese which makes these substantial commitments on the part of the host difficult to understand, unless examined closely. As we will show in subsequent chapters, bid commitments are often glossed over, if referenced at all, during debates surrounding the value of bidding within the host community. This is despite the significant impact these guarantees may have on public spaces, freedom of expression and commercial operations within the host for the duration of the event.

In addition, these guarantees will invariably include documents outlining technical, professional or managerial elements. For example, the UK City of Culture bid instructions (DCMS, 2013) include requirements for risk assessments, whilst the Commonwealth Games Federation, in its candidate guidelines for the 2018 Games (won by Gold Coast) required information regarding issues such as medical and health services and security from prospective candidates. Despite smaller events heavily restricting the size of candidate files in an effort to reduce costs to bidding nations (see DCMS, 2013), and major organisations such as the IOC encouraging brevity in their submissions (Masterman, 2009), these documents are hugely complex and require significant investment of time and money from candidate cities. Such is the level of input required to meet these technical elements that it is little surprise small-scale bids can require hundreds of thousands of pounds of investment. For example Leicester, England, spent £125,000 on its failed 2017 UK City of Culture bid; whilst sporting mega event bids can run into the tens of millions, such as the £21 million spent by England when attempting to host the 2018 FIFA World Cup.

Regardless of the event, a detailed financial plan is also required. In the case of sporting mega events such as the Olympics, this includes full details on the cost of the Games and the full candidature process (Masterman, 2009). The intention of this element is to ensure that cost estimates are realistic and a clear plan is in place for

the delivery of the event. However, similar to other areas of the bidding documentation, this element can also enshrine serious commitments on the part of the
prospective host. In the guidelines for the 2017 UK City of Culture (DCMS,
2013), the financial instructions include the key question, "What evidence is there
of commitment to meet the funding gap and act as guarantor?" (p.21), whereas the
Commonwealth Games Federation require "a financial guarantee from the competent
authorities covering a potential economic shortfall of the OC" (Commonwealth
Games Federation, 2011:50). Here, in a manner replicated for most sporting mega
events, the bid team are committing, at this earliest stage in the process, to underwrite
any financial loss with public funds. Given Whitson & Horne's (2006) oft-noted sug-
gestion that sporting mega events are typically characterised by massively under-
estimated costs, this can represent dangerous territory for a prospective host,
particularly in the case of Olympic Games which, as Flyvbjerg & Stewart (2012) suggest, run, on average, 179% over budget. However, awareness of this commitment
and its potential ramifications for the host is typically low during the bidding process.
Indeed, often, financial predictions around such events are highly positive. Lauermann's (2016) analysis of Boston's bid for the 2024 Olympics is typical of this, highlighting a bid proclamation that the proposed budget would not require a dollar of tax
payers' money. This claim was subsequently proven to be inaccurate by anti-bid activists within the city, which promised public funding for a range of Olympic projects
and requirements. Again, transparency and accountability become key watchwords in
the world of Olympic bidding, a theme which will be discussed further in Chapter 8.

The bid documentation also requires candidates to address the physical aspects of
delivery, providing information on areas such as venues, accommodation and transport
infrastructure. Again in the case of a sporting mega event, this can be a wide-ranging
and detailed process, requiring highly technical information, "from planning
through to permanent construction, overlay operations, transition to Paralympic
Games (where applicable) and retrofit" (IOC, 2013:50). Further to this, sporting
mega event awarding bodies request detailed overviews of the quantity, quality and
location of accommodation made available to athletes, delegates, media and spectators,
with events such as the Commonwealth Games seeking guarantees in the form of a
"Statement from your national tourist board describing your country's hotel rating
system and candidate city hotel room inventory. List of the candidate city's total
hotel room capacity, guaranteed by the national tourist board" (Commonwealth
Games Federation, 2011:112). This demand for information is reflected across a
range of other areas with detailed information required on transport, where issues
such as travel times between venues, international and domestic travel routes and
guarantees regarding traffic management systems, such as London 2012's controversial 'Olympic Lanes' are all required. Even smaller undertakings such as bidding to be a European Capital of Culture place a requirement on prospective hosts
to demonstrate:

> that the tourist and visitor capacity of the city can cope within the targets set
> out in the plan. This covers not only hotel capacity, transport links etc. but

also the soft skill areas of visitor languages, quality of hospitality and welcome programmes (both in the public and private sectors) available in the city.

(European Commission, 2014:11)

Of all aspects of the bidding process, the physical infrastructural requirements are perhaps the most widely criticised. Significant literature exists condemning the venue arms race which has been the hallmark of major events in recent years. Whitson & Horne (2006) highlight Nagano's 1998 Winter Olympics barely used 'Nagano Spiral' and massively expensive 'M–Wave' facilities, whilst Barclay (2009) highlights the $6 billion committed to the construction of venues in Japan and Korea ahead of the 2002 FIFA World Cup to meet FIFA's requirement of at least eight venues capable of hosting 40,000 to 60,000 spectators. More recently, Brazil's 2014 FIFA World Cup bid saw the construction of several stadia best described as 'white elephants', including the $300 million Arena Amazonia in Manaus, located hundreds of miles from any significant population centre and the $550 million Estadio Nacional in Brasilia which, within one year of the Finals, was being used as a parking lot for buses. Looking to forthcoming events, Baumann & Matheson (2013) highlight Qatar's commitment to building ten 45,000 seater stadiums as part of their bid for the 2022 FIFA World Cup. A significant commitment for a nation with a population of just 2.5 million. In each case, the requirements of the awarding body can be seen to take precedence and overrule the development needs of the host.

This criticism has led to significant revision and reflection on bidding processes in recent years, with a greater emphasis placed on bids which are more sustainable and give greater consideration to the post-event value and utilisation of these venues, with the IOC bid criteria for the 2022 Winter Olympics attempting to direct candidates away from promises of new venues by instructing, "build a new permanent venue only if there is a legacy need, ensuring flexible use if possible" (IOC, 2013:50). Likewise, the decision by UEFA to host the 2020 European Championships across multiple cities across the continent rather than one single nation was argued to be a step towards removing the financial burden on one single host nation. In response to significant critique in this area, among others, 2014 saw the IOC produce a new *Olympic Agenda 2020* (International Olympic Committee, 2014) to deliver, among other improvements, more sustainable bidding processes and, by extension, Games. Similarly, following significant allegations of corruption, FIFA suspended the bidding process for the 2026 FIFA World Cup and pledged a more sustainable model for future events. However, despite these claims towards a more sustainable approach, it is worth highlighting that massive infrastructure investment is still seen as a key part of bidding strategies. Guidelines for the European Capital of Culture (European Commission, 2014) still highlight the "major infrastructure developments" (p.11) of successful candidates such as Marseilles, France (2013) and Plzen, Czech Republic (2015) in a manner which implies a route to a successful bid, and the IOC awarded the above mentioned 2022 Winter Olympics to Beijing despite the likely need to transport vast amounts of snow, at huge costs financially and environmentally, to venues which could not guarantee the required snowfall for the event, highlighting Müller's (2015) assertion that sporting mega events led to a development agenda which focusses on the successful delivery of the event over the sustainable development of the host city or nation.

Finally, in addition to the hard physical infrastructure requirements, some demonstration of the soft infrastructure and intangible skills required to successfully host the event must be demonstrated in the bidding documentation. The guidelines for the UK City of Culture (DCMS, 2013) ask simply, "How strong is the track record in delivering significant programmes of events?" (p.21). Masterman (2009) highlights that for the IOC, prospective cities must provide detailed information on the last ten major events hosted within the previous ten years. This is intended to protect the delivery of the event itself but also, in principle, to ensure that the prospective host is realistic in their bidding ambitions and do not over-reach. This is reflected in the bid feedback for Aberdeen's bid to be UK City of Culture in 2017, which suggested the city's lack of experience in hosting events of a similar scale meant it was unable to make a compelling case regarding the deliverability of the event (Regeneris, 2013). Similarly, and many years earlier, Libya's lack of experience proved fatal to their hopes of securing the 2010 FIFA World Cup, as serious doubts were raised in the FIFA Inspection documentation regarding their ability to host the event without the need to import overseas expertise (FIFA, 2004). The result of this need to demonstrate experience is that many cities and nations will bid for and stage several smaller events with a view towards eventually bidding for the ultimate prize of a sporting mega event. However, it can also be seen as leading to serial bidding from cities and nations which seek to use a previous bidding cycle as evidence of having developed the requisite experience of hosting a future iteration. Rio, Paris and Istanbul have all returned to the Olympic bidding arena shortly after unsuccessful bids, whilst at a national level, countries such as the UK, the USA and Australia have made multiple bids from various cities in quick succession, based on the notion of institutional memory providing strength and demonstrating this much desired 'experience'.

Evaluations and inspections

Once completed, the bidding documentation must be evaluated by the awarding body. This element of the process is, again, considerably under-examined in the current literature surrounding major events; and, once again, the exact criteria used differ significantly from one awarding body and indeed one event cycle to another, with some of the exact detail not readily publicly available. This renders a line-by-line description of the process difficult and lacking in value. However, as before, general trends can be identified and critiqued in order to gain some deeper understanding of the process. Broadly, evaluations of a prospective host can be seen to involve a detailed scoring of the bid document itself, typically supported by a form of inspection visit or evaluation.

In the context of the Olympic Games, this process is governed by an Evaluation Commission, tasked by the sitting President of the IOC with examining the candidature of the competing prospective hosts and advising the IOC Session, Executive and President on all matters pertaining to the bid at each stage of the process. In the context of FIFA, a similar process has governed recent bidding processes competitions for major events, with an Evaluation Group reviewing each bidding nation's documents and following this with an inspection visit. Similarly, the Commonwealth Games Federation appoints an Evaluation Commission which reviews the bid documentation and then stages an inspection visit prior to the announcement of the winning bid. In each case, the evaluation group can be seen to mirror the composition of bid committees within the host destination. They typically draw upon a range of expertise from across the relevant aspects of event organisation. The IOC Evaluation Commission, as an example, contains IOC members, National Olympic Committee members, representatives of the Athletes' Commission and the International Paralympic Committee, as well as a range of technical experts able to comment upon the various required elements of a bid. For smaller events, where a standing pool of technical experts do not exist, it may be the case that an independent consultancy firm provides the technical expertise in evaluation before reporting to an appointed board who make the final decision. This can be seen in the case of the UK City of Culture award where an independent consultant, Regeneris Consulting, conducted the initial bid assessment before allowing an independent panel appointed by the DCMS and consisting of a range of renowned figures in the UK's cultural sector to bestow the final award. These committees will typically visit each potential host for a number of days and use this period to tour facilities and venues, meet with key staff associated with the bid, receive presentations regarding the candidate's proposals and evaluate intangible aspects such as 'host community support'.

Following inspection visits, the committees typically then publish, in the public domain, evaluative reports outlining their findings to the awarding body. In many cases, little detail is given on how this evaluation is graded and scored, if at all. Evaluations for the 2018 FIFA World Cup, as an example, typically begin with the claim, "we feel we have accomplished our work in the spirit of integrity, objectiveness and transparency" (FIFA, 2010:2). However, a review of the documentation reveals little quantification of the feedback in relation to each aspect of the evaluation process. Whilst individual sections of evaluation reports make concluding statements, there is little in the way of overall evaluation and assessment in the documentation. The evaluation reports include 'annexe' elements which provide a risk assessment of the various legal and operational aspects of delivery, but these are brief in note and make use of a simplistic high/medium/low risk evaluation system. The result of this lengthy process is documents which make no definitive statement on capacity and capability, leaving the FIFA Executive Committee, which vote upon the final award, with substantial room for interpretation in their deliberations, introducing, as Chapters 5 and 6 will demonstrate in depth, space for intangible factors to influence this final decision.

In contrast, the IOC makes use of a clearer grading system in its evaluative reports. As outlined in the candidature process for the 2018 Winter Olympics

(IOC, 2010), each criteria detailed in the bid documentation is evaluated on a scale from 0 to 10 ranging from 'unsatisfactory' to 'satisfactory', with weightings given to each element of the criteria. This allows, in principle, for a direct comparison between prospective hosts and evaluation of their comparable technical competency. However, the process is muddied by the actual process of awarding a grade in each category as each candidate is awarded not one but two numbers in each element. The bid guidelines outline this process as follows: "A grade (on a case of 0 to 10) was given to each criteria, comprising a minimum and maximum number. The more uncertain a criterion's grade, the wider the span between the minimum and maximum grade" (IOC, 2010:6).

The result of this can be wide margins of error for evaluating candidates. For example, Annecy's failed bid for the same Games was scored as between 4 and 7 in the category of 'Overall Concept', a wide range on a narrow grading criterion. In addition, the use of minimum and maximum criteria makes it difficult to draw a clear conclusion as to which bid is technically, quantifiably 'better'. Despite being evaluated on a wide range of criteria, both Munich and eventual host Pyeongchang were considered to have equal bids, both scoring between 8 or 9 for overall concept. This was despite Munich being noticeably stronger when graded on seemingly key individual elements such as general infrastructure, sport venues, environmental conditions and previous experience. Despite the use of clearly stated grading criteria, it is still difficult to pinpoint exactly which bid is strongest, something which is, we argue, intentional from the outset, with the evaluation group clear to "re-emphasize that its task is not to suggest any final judgement on which city should host the 2018 Winter Olympic Games" (IOC, 2010:61). Again, this element of the bidding process, therefore, rather than being objective and clear, affords the awarding body a veneer of transparency whilst allowing for a range of other factors to influence the final decision.

The bid process: the 2024 Summer Olympic Games

At the time of writing, the most current sporting mega event bidding process is the Candidature Process [for the] Olympic Games 2024 (see IOC, 2015). This process, which officially began in September 2015, is scheduled to conclude in September 2017 with the election of the host city at the IOC Session in Peru, with Los Angeles and Paris currently in the running to host the Games. The 2024 Candidature Process has proven to be one of the most controversial in recent memory, with Hamburg, Rome and Budapest all withdrawing after being confirmed as candidate cities. In the case of Hamburg, this followed a public referendum which saw 51.6% of citizens reject the bid, and in Rome, this followed the election of a new Mayor, Virginia Raggi, who had campaigned against the city's candidature due to concerns regarding the financial implications of hosting the event. Budapest's withdrawal, in February 2017, followed a public petition, signed by over 250,000 citizens demanding the cancellation of the bid. Earlier in the process a range of cities, most notably Boston, abandoned prospective bids due to citizen protests and anti-Olympic movements. This was despite the 2024 Candidature Process being the first Summer Games awarded under the guidelines of *Olympic Agenda 2020* (IOC, 2014) which was designed to create a fairer and more transparent process and enable cities to engage with the IOC as prospective candidates at a more significant level.

In addition to linking closely to the new *Olympic 2020 Agenda*, the Candidature Process is designed to foster a more co-operative relationship between prospective hosts and the IOC, developing a dialogue and allowing for both collaboration and information exchange. The intention of this process is to create bids which align closely with long-term development plans within candidate cities and ensure a significant focus upon sustainability and legacy. To support this, prior to the official Candidature Process beginning in earnest, the IOC held an invitation phase between March and September 2015. This phase enabled interested cities to engage in an ongoing dialogue with the IOC regarding the viability of hosting the Games without making a commitment to become candidate cities, incurring the cost and legal implications of this formalisation of candidature. This invitation phase sees the IOC assist prospective hosts to "better shape their value proposition" (IOC, 2015:13) and, in principle, is designed to reduce speculative and costly 'alibi' bids or bids which are likely to be highly unsustainable and therefore unsuccessful.

Following this, the formal Candidature Process begins with each National Organising Committee wishing to formally become a candidate city writing to the IOC in September 2015. For 2024, this is a three-stage process, each requiring specific information regarding an element of the Games and a significant financial commitment on the part of the candidate.

The first stage of this process (see International Olympic Committee, 2015), *Vision, Games Concept and Strategy*, requires the prospective candidate to outline key information regarding the overall vision of the Games, including elements such as venue and Olympic Village concepts, but also elements such as potential dates and weather conditions. This stage also requires a detailed outline of the long-term development plan for the host city and how the Games articulate with this approach. Basic general infrastructure and capacity information is also required at this stage in the process, along with a Candidature Service Fee of $50,000. The second stage of the process, *Governance, Legal and Venue Funding*, focusses upon demonstrating institutional support for the Games within the candidate city, and requires the submission of expressions of support and a range of guarantees which reflect this commitment. These guarantees cover areas such as taxes, ambush marketing, governance promises, host country entry regulations and Games workforce regulations. At this stage a further $50,000 Candidature Service Fee is also required. The final stage of the process, *Games Delivery, Experience and Venue Legacy*, centres around a Games project analysis which gives consideration to the delivery risks and opportunities posed by the hosting of the event. Candidates must give a detailed outline of the specific delivery risks, but also outline sustainable solutions to these challenges. During this stage, notions of legacy come to the forefront and candidates must give detailed plans for engaging the host community and visitors during and after the Games. In addition, this stage of the process requires a detailed outline of the candidate city's experience of hosting major events and preparedness to manage the complexity of the Games proposed. This includes giving a more detailed plan for the delivery of the Games in terms of dates, facilities and the management of athlete experience. Candidates progressing to this stage of the process must also pay a final Candidature Service Fee of $150,000.

As mentioned previously, in a departure from previous Candidature Processes, and in a bid to produce a more sustainable bid process, the IOC supports each stage of the bid process with workshops designed to help each individual candidate improve their bid and ensure progress to the next stage of the process. This is further supported by the IOC Observer Programme, a tailor-made programme for prospective hosts which enabled them to attend the Rio 2016 Games and learn first-hand from the Rio Organising Committee in real time during the delivery of the 2016 Olympiad and the Official Debriefing of the Olympic Games Rio 2016, held in Tokyo in November 2016. These knowledge-transfer events are intended to act as a learning platform for prospective hosts and to enable them to maximise the success of future Games. These events also include opportunities for candidates to present to, and network with, IOC members in carefully controlled environments designed to reduce candidate costs and increase transparency in the bid process. (See Chapter 7 for more on this.) Finally, the 2024 Candidature Process is supported by the development of "shaRing", an information portal open to all candidate cities, designed to act as a 'one-stop-shop' for the sharing of materials relating to the bid process, including access to information regarding previous Games.

Following these three stages, candidate cities receive a delegation of IOC members in the form of the IOC Evaluation Committee. This Committee undertakes a visit of two to three days designed to examine the suitability of the candidate and evaluate the quality of their facilities, infrastructure and plans. Following the publication of their Evaluation Reports for each candidate city, the final election of the Host City takes place at the IOC Session in Lima in September 2017.

Conclusion

This chapter has laid out the technical process of bidding for major events. It has demonstrated the complexity of this process, the importance of bringing together the correct group of people and the challenges of delivering the detailed documentation required to convince an awarding body of the value of giving hosting rights to a particular candidate. We have also laid out the process by which these bids are evaluated and the results of this process, such as it may be, communicated to awarding bodies. However, what we have ultimately attempted to outline in this chapter are the vagaries which underpin so much of the bidding process, even in the supposedly transparent and technical elements such as those discussed here. Starting from bidding committees formed without oversight and shaped in such a way as to reduce dissent and potentially even manufacture consent for a bid, moving through to bid documentation which shapes specific legal and financial commitments in a broad language open to (re)interpretation; the technical process of bidding for a major event is steeped in uncertainties and a double speak which enables candidates to make significant promises to awarding bodies without alienating home audiences. Similarly, evaluation processes speak a language of transparency and objectivity, whilst creating criteria vague enough to allow for the final decision to be made around a series of intangible factors and away from the public light of scrutiny. In conclusion, it would appear that the technical components of the bidding process offer a level of uncertainty which allows for decisions to be made seemingly on the basis of technical evidence, but which are actually based upon a series of other factors. The following chapters move on to examine these other, intangible factors and their impact on the bidding process in more detail.

References

Aberdeen 2017 (2013) *Illuminating the North.* Aberdeen: Aberdeen City Council.

Balibrea, M.P. (2001) Urbanism, culture and the post-industrial city: Challenging the 'Barcelona model'. *Journal of Spanish Cultural Studies,* 2(2), pp.187–210.

Barclay, J. (2009) Predicting the costs and benefits of mega-sporting events: Misjudgement of Olympic proportions? *Economic Affairs,* 29(2), pp.62–66.

Baumann, R. and Matheson, V. (2013) *Infrastructure investments and mega-sports events: Comparing the experience of developing and industrialized countries.* Economics Department Working Papers. Paper 147.

Commonwealth Games Federation (2011) *Candidate city manual 2018 Commonwealth Games.* London: Commonwealth Games Federation.

Department for Culture, Media and Sport (DCMS) (2013) *UK City of Culture 2017: Guidance for bidding cities.* London: DCMS.

European Commission (2014) *European Capitals of Culture 2020–2033: Guide for cities preparing to bid.* Brussels: European Commission.

FIFA (2004) *Inspection group report for the 2010 FIFA World Cup.* Switzerland: FIFA.

FIFA (2010) *2018 bid evaluation report: Russia.* Switzerland: FIFA.

Flyvbjerg, B. and Stewart, A. (2012) *Olympic proportions: Cost and cost overrun at the Olympics 1960–2012.* (1 June 2012). Saïd Business School Working Papers, 23. Oxford: University of Oxford.

Foley, M., McGillivray, D. and McPherson, G. (2012) *Event policy: From theory to strategy.* London: Routledge.

Griffiths, E. (2000) *Bidding for glory: Why South Africa lost the Olympic and World Cup bids, and how to win next time.* Johannesburg: Jonathan Ball Publishers.

Hiller, H.H. (2000) Mega-events, urban boosterism and growth strategies: An analysis of the objectives and legitimations of the Cape Town 2004 Olympic Bid. *International Journal of Urban & Regional Research,* 24(2), pp.449–458.

International Olympic Committee (2008) *2016 candidature procedure and questionnaire.* Lausanne: IOC.

International Olympic Committee (2010) *Report of the IOC 2018 Evaluation Commission.* Lausanne: IOC.

International Olympic Committee (2013) *2022 candidate acceptance procedure.* Lausanne: IOC. Available at https://stillmed.olympic.org/Documents/Host_city_elections/2022-Candidature-Acceptance-Procedure-FINAL-with-cover.pdf (accessed 7 July 2017).

International Olympic Committee (2014) *Olympic agenda 2020: 20+20 recommendations.* Lausanne: IOC.

International Olympic Committee (2015) *Candidature process Olympic Games 2024*. Lausanne: IOC.

Lauermann, J. (2016) Boston's Olympic bid and the evolving urban politics of event-led development. *Urban Geography*, 37(2), pp.313–321.

Lenskyj, H.J. (2008) *Olympic industry resistance: Challenging Olympic power and propaganda*. Albany: SUNY Press.

Masterman, G. (2009) *Strategic sports event management*. Olympic edn. Amsterdam: Elsevier Butterworth-Heinemann.

Mitchell, R.K., Agle, B.R. and Wood, D.J. (1997) Toward a theory of stakeholder identification and salience: Defining the principle of who and what really counts. *Academy of Management Review*, 22(4), pp.853–886.

Mooney, G. (2004) Cultural policy as urban transformation? Critical reflections on Glasgow, European City of Culture 1990. *Local Economy*, 19(4), pp.327–340.

Müller, M. (2015) The mega-event syndrome: Why so much goes wrong in mega-event planning and what to do about it. *Journal of the American Planning Association*, 81(1), pp.6–17.

Regeneris (2013) Aberdeen: Initial bid for the UK City of Culture. Available at http://www.aberdeencity.gov.uk/nmsruntime/saveasdialog.asp?lID=51566&sID=26376 (accessed 22 December 2016).

Richards, G. and Palmer, R. (2010) *Eventful cities*. London: Routledge.

Shaw, C.A. (2008) *Five ring circus: Myths and realities of the Olympic Games*. British Columbia: New Society Publishers.

Theodoraki, E. (2007) *Olympic event organization*. London: Routledge.

Westerbeek, H.M., Turner, P. and Ingerson, L. (2002) Key success factors in bidding for hallmark sporting events. *International Marketing Review*, 19(3), pp.303–322.

Whitson, D. and Horne, J. (2006) Part 2. The glocal politics of sports mega-events: Underestimated costs and overestimated benefits? Comparing the outcomes of sports mega-events in Canada and Japan. *The Sociological Review*, 54(s2), pp.71–89.

5

BIDDING NARRATIVES

Positioning through storytelling

Introduction

> As competition to host sports events is becoming much fiercer, it is no longer enough to simply meet the requirements of the event specification. The bidding city must offer something more. In order to win over the evaluators, the media and the decision makers it is often necessary to add a strong emotional and/or cultural element to the bid.
>
> *(Brighenti, Clivaz, Délétroz & Favre, 2005:52)*

As Brighenti et al. (2005) highlight, event bids must increasingly give consideration to more than simply those technical elements of the bidding process discussed in the previous chapter. Bidding processes have become more competitive and more demanding in terms of the requirements of awarding bodies, and candidate cities or nations have increasingly responded by professionalising their bid campaigns. This professionalisation has been achieved through the formation of more experienced bid teams, and, as a result the development of bid documentation and activities which demonstrate a keener understanding of the technical requirements of a bid process.

This, coupled with the high cost of staging a bid, means that even 'alibi' bid (Masterman, 2009) candidates are highly unlikely to enter bidding contests unless they are able to meet the basic technical requirements of hosting their chosen event. Whilst Griffiths (2000) highlights the "chaotic and confused" (p.91) bids from a range of African nations ahead of the 2006 FIFA World Cup, increasingly, the list of candidates for hosting major peripatetic events will contain only those prospective hosts capable of clearly demonstrating the base level of technical expertise required for successful delivery. This is best demonstrated by the bid process for the 2024 Olympic Games which attracted serious bids only from major cities in Central Europe (Budapest, Hamburg, Rome, Paris) and North America (Los Angeles).

Separately to this, fuelled by events such as the election of Donald Trump in the USA and the Brexit referendum in the UK, there is an increasing interest in the notion we live in a 'post-truth' era. The *Oxford English Dictionary*, in selecting post-truth as its international word of the year, argued the term saw a 2,000% increase in usage in 2016. In a post-truth era, discussions around socio-political issues see substance and detail replaced with an emphasis on rhetoric and narrative. Increasingly, storytelling becomes a central theme of contemporary life. Rojek (2013) engages with this notion when asking "why are events so emotional?" (p.139). He explores the growth of participatory resistant events (such as Live 8) and suggests that participation in these events allows a pseudo-resistance, where representation acts as a form of resistance in place of real engagement. This storytelling phenomenon extends into the world of sporting mega events. Peña, de Moragas, Lallana & Rezende (2010) discuss opening ceremonies of sporting mega events as a storytelling apparatus for the host nation to produce and disseminate an image of the nation to the world. McGillivray (2014) highlights how individuals increasingly engage in digital storytelling, capturing and documenting their landmark moments, such as interactions with major events, via social media. We posit that this post-truth storytelling also exists in the event bidding world. Decisions on the awarding of hosting rights now invariably centre on less tangible variables. Frequently, a successful bid will make use of an emotional 'narrative' to supplement its professional-technical competency and to convince awarding bodies to choose it over other similarly technically capable candidates. Cornelissen (2004) suggests that these narratives are best understood as a combination of stories, ideologies and claims used to legitimise and support the bid campaign. They are also employed to generate support for the candidate over competing bids, directing the gaze away from rational, technical criteria and onto more subjective components. In this chapter we outline how these processes work, both in theory and practice. We identify two principal bid strategies used by candidate cities or nations: *reward* and *scholarship*. The premise of this chapter is simple: bidding processes and award decisions are not rational. The 'best' bid, in terms of technical competence and professional capability, does not always translate into the winning bid. Successful bids make use of emotive rhetoric and clever storytelling narratives to supplement their technical competence and gain support. In addition, we argue that bidding processes are multidimensional, with successful candidates recognising that a bid need not only be positioned solely in response to the stated bid criteria. Rather, bids compete tactically against, and in response to, competitors in the bid process. Finally, we examine the historical context in which bidding contests are situated, emphasising the need to understand not just how a bid is situated in reference to the specific iteration of the event it seeks to host, but also to the recent history of that event, in general.

Reward narratives

The first significant narrative type that can be identified in bids is that of *reward*. This is typically the narrative of the front-runner. The reward narrative works on a simple premise – that the bidder in question is the candidate that best meets the technical requirements of the bid process and should be 'rewarded' for doing so by winning the rights to host the event. Reward narratives have received little academic attention, however, a clear parallel can be drawn with Black's (2007) discussion of 'cosmopolitanism' in event bids. Black's (2007) examination of Vancouver's ultimately successful bid for the 2010 Winter Olympics highlights how the city positioned itself as a "safe and secure bet for a well-managed event" (p.268) as well as emphasising the diverse, multi-cultural nature of the city's population. Although ultimately unsuccessful, Shoval (2002) highlights how New York's bid for the 2012 Summer Olympics drew upon its existing capability and capacity to host a sporting mega event with little development of the city's urban infrastructure. At a national, rather than global level, Leicester's bid to be 2017 UK City of Culture centred around the diversity of its cultural offering, highlighting the quality and variety of its performance spaces and range of festivities, positioning the city as a thriving cultural centre deserving of coronation.

Bids that exemplify reward narratives emphasise the existing capacity of the city or nation to deliver the event and appeal to the need for certainty and guaranteed return on investment for awarding bodies. Typically, these bids will make reference to their previous track record of hosting major events as a justification for their capacity, capability and competence to host the event in question. Often, this is part of a cumulative process whereby successful hosting of smaller events become stepping stones supporting the final bid for a larger event. Glasgow's successful bid for the 2014 Commonwealth Games made significant use of this strategy, with the city highlighting its successful hosting of national or international championship-level events in each of the Commonwealth sports as evidence of its ability to successfully host the Games. Indeed, Stell (2014) highlights how Glasgow positioned the Games as the culmination of a thirty-year renaissance within the city which had, during that period, repositioned itself as an 'events city'. Interestingly, Masterman (2009) highlights how many countries have used unsuccessful Olympic bids as a catalyst to produce subsequent, stronger bids which have proven successful. In such cases, being a prior bidder legitimises the candidature and gives the impression of a considered, well-planned bid likely to lead to a similarly well-coordinated event. However, the reward narrative is often the preserve of the western, first-world cities and nations who historically have dominated hosting rights for sporting mega events. For example, reward was a noticeable motif in Chicago's unsuccessful 2016 Olympic Games bid, which emphasised a long-term planning strategy stretching back to the 1909 Plan of Chicago. Additionally, Germany's successful candidature for the 2006 FIFA World Cup was explicitly linked to a twelve-year destination development strategy, giving the perception of a well-considered, carefully developed bid from an established candidate (Grix, 2012). As Shoval's (2002) work demonstrates, candidates often bid, not for developmental reasons, but rather to reinforce their position as leading cities and nations – with the event award acting as global recognition for that feat. Whilst reference will be made to redevelopment projects, such as London's emphasis on the physical transformation of the city's East

End, the core purpose of bidding is to articulate a view of the candidate as a leading light, and bids utilising the reward narrative reflect this in their confident articulation of the candidate as the rightful heir to the event.

Scholarship narratives

In contrast to reward narratives, those of *scholarship* are often the preserve of the underdog candidate. The use of such strategies has been discussed more extensively than that of reward strategies (see Cornelissen, 2004) but it is still an under-researched area. Typically, scholarship narratives focus on the act of 'becoming' or, to use Black's (2007) term "transcendence" (p.262). Cities and nations bidding under this strategy attempt to reframe the bidding process, carefully introducing an emotional element which is intended to move award decisions away from a reliance on 'hard', technical competencies and instead towards 'softer', more intangible considerations. Those making use of the scholarship narrative focus upon the transformations – tangible or intangible – that would be achieved in the candidate city or nation as a result of being awarded the event. The exact nature of the emotional rhetoric advanced differs depending on the economic and geo-political context of the bidding nation. For example, Cornelissen (2004) has shown how African bids for the 2006 and 2010 FIFA World Cup events, most notably from South Africa and Morocco, played on the notion that the African continent had long been neglected by the Western world and that it was 'Africa's turn' to benefit from hosting the Finals. Stell (2014) identifies a similar theme in Abuja's failed bid to host the 2014 Commonwealth Games, a bid which highlighted the lack of a previous Games on African soil and claimed hosting the 2014 edition was either a "right or a privilege" (p.6). The notion that hosting a major sporting event is a right of global citizenship has been a strong element of the bids of other prospective first-time host cities and nations in recent years. Both Rio (2016, Summer Olympic Games) and Qatar (2022, FIFA World Cup) emphasised their role as first time hosts within their regions in bid documentation. However, it is Alegi (2001) who emphasises this most clearly when examining South Africa's bid to host the FIFA World Cup:

> The new 'Feel the Pull in Your Soul' motto of 1999 conveyed the argument that South Africa should get the World Cup because "the West had a moral obligation toward a nation emerging from decades of apartheid, where soccer is the passion of the long-oppressed black majority".
>
> *(p.9)*

The implication of this message was clear – if the IOC and FIFA were truly representative of a global community then they had an obligation to take their events to all corners of that globe. In terms of 'second-order' events (Black, 2008), Kuala Lumpur's campaign slogan for its successful bid for the 1998 Commonwealth Games also highlighted this approach, imploring the Commonwealth Games Federation to "Share it with Malaysia" (Stell, 2014:3).

Other candidates have made use of a scholarship narrative in alternative ways, focussing on the event as a means of transforming the host locale. For example, as explored in Chapter 3, bids from 'transition economies' (Humphreys & Prokopo-wicz, 2007) explicitly make clear their intention to use a successful bid as a springboard for development in the economic, environmental, political and socio-cultural spheres of civic life. Cornelissen & Swart (2006) make note of the "developmental philosophy" (p.110) which underpinned Cape Town's unsuc-cessful bid for the 2004 Summer Olympic Games and Alegi (2001) notes a similar development agenda within the narrative of the nation's successful bid for the 2006 FIFA World Cup. In the cultural sphere, Liverpool's successful bid to be European Capital of Culture in 2008 was predicated heavily on a message of eco-nomic instrumentalism and holistic regeneration, which would see the city com-plete its journey through post-industrial decline and towards a future as a creative and cultural hub (Connolly, 2013). Liverpool's 2008 European Capital of Culture bid represents an exemplar of a prospective host that promoted a 'becoming' narrative, making it clear that the award would help bring about improvements in cultural opportunities for a range of publics in that city. More recently, within the same city, a bid for the 2026 Commonwealth Games has been articulated as being a potential "catalyst for regeneration" (*Liverpool Echo*, 2016 [online]). Scharfenort (2012) notes a similar theme within Qatar's successful bid for the 2022 FIFA World Cup, highlighting the event as being a centrepiece of the Gulf state's strategic vision for 2030, making a contribution to a range of areas including the economy, built infrastructure and global political capital. Both Liverpool and Qatar's successful bids highlight the power of utilising a scholarship narrative to enable an unlikely candidate to prevail in a bidding contest. In the case of Liverpool (see below), the city used a scholarship narrative to paint its bid as a means to promote itself as a modern destination city with a thriving multi-dimensional cultural sector.

In the case of Qatar, the Gulf state's bid managed to realign its bid campaign away from serious concerns regarding its capacity and capability to hold the event given the size and climate of the nation (Scharfenort, 2012). Recognising it would surely have failed in such a circumstance, Qatar instead refocussed the bid campaign around a scholarship narrative which emphasised economic, social and environmental development, and combined this with an aspirational narrative, which showcased technological innovation in venue design and event delivery. This final example is, of course, somewhat caveated by the subsequent allegations and evidence of mass corruption surrounding this particular campaign (Brannagan & Giulianotti, 2015; Dorsey, 2014) which cast serious doubt on exactly why FIFA delegates were willing to be swayed by this strategy, a theme examined further in Chapter 7. However, the nature of the narrative employed, despite how it may have been supported and actioned, demonstrates a textbook 'scholarship' approach.

Liverpool 08 – European Capital of Culture: scholarship in action

In 2003, Liverpool secured the European Capital of Culture title, unexpectedly beating competition from Birmingham, Bristol, Oxford, Cardiff and Newcastle-Gateshead. Whilst Liverpool had a strong cultural history, particularly in terms of its physical infrastructure and its links to The Beatles, the city was widely expected to fall short in the final judgement (Little, 2008). From the shortlisting stage through to the bid announcement, the city was expected to lose out to Newcastle-Gateshead's bid, which boasted an ambitious capital projects plan including landmark facilities such as the Baltic Art Gallery, Sage Concert Hall and the Millennium Bridge and had already attracted international attention (*The Guardian*, 2002). Other competitors such as Oxford and Birmingham claimed superiority through 'reward' bids, which emphasised international reputation or size and global prominence. So, whilst Liverpool's shortlisting made sense given its strong history, an overall victory felt unlikely. In hindsight, this underdog tag became a key part of Liverpool's bid and the city used that status to develop a 'scholarship' strategy to underpin its candidature. Throughout the bidding process the city emphasised the need for a project which would "regenerate a city that had been on its knees" (Jones, 2013 [online]). At the heart of this campaign was the message that the city would forge a new identity as a result of a successful bid (Platt, 2011), one which would allow the city to move past the economic decline and political unrest which dominated Liverpool in the 1970s and 1980s (Little, 2008). This underdog status was developed despite the city being the recipient of significant European funding in the years before the event, much of which was used to develop the backbone of cultural infrastructure which underpinned the European Capital of Culture bid itself (Cox & O'Brien, 2012).

At the heart of this underdog, *scholarship* narrative was the idea that Liverpool's bid was one which would have greater impact upon the 'real people' of the city, in comparison to competitors elsewhere. García, Melville & Cox (2010) highlight that the city made ambitious promises during the bid campaign regarding the ability of the year of culture to transform the economic and social circumstances of the city, with Connolly (2013) characterising the bid as being not about culture but rather regeneration. Central to this, as Platt (2011) highlights, was an internal campaign, convincing the people of Liverpool themselves that 2008 should be supported on the premise that it was "Our Time, Our Place" (p.34). Connolly (2013) highlights how this campaign to galvanise host community support saw Liverpool position its bid as 'The People's Bid', one which attempted to generate a significant amount of community engagement and public investment in the campaign, with a range or projects such as 'Bottle Your Culture'; an event which saw Liverpudlians express their culture by creating bottles of personal artefacts, designed to create a range of activities which both engaged the local population in the bid and helped strengthen the city's carefully constructed public relations message of 'the world in one city'. This 'people's bid' narrative translated into other activities in the bid campaign with a focus placed on encouraging judges and visitors to visit the city to meet 'real people' rather than 'men in suits and businessmen' (Doran in Jones, 2013). Throughout the campaign, recognising the growing importance of social and cultural legacies, Liverpool successfully developed a narrative to convince the judging panel that its bid was borne of the unique circumstance of people and place and would, crucially, transform the city. Ultimately, this approach proved to be the key factor in the city's success, with the chair of the judges' panel, Sir Jeremy Isaacs, explaining that Liverpool was chosen as a result of developing a greater sense "that the whole city is involved in and behind the bid" (BBC News, 2003 [online]).

Positioning the bid

Potential hosts can combine both the obligation and development aspects of a scholarship strategy. For example, prospective first time hosts in developing economies (see for example Rio 2016 and South Africa 2010) often seek to combine elements of both a reward and a scholarship narrative in order to produce a compelling emotional message, combining both push and pull motivations for awarding bodies. These strategies play to the vanity of awarding bodies, casting them in the light of generous benefactor, bequeathing their event and its transformative power to the lucky host. This narrative plays on the irrationality of the bidding process. For all the technical reports, detailed bid criteria and refined, logical processes which are laid out in an attempt to give bidding contests a veneer of objective impartiality, the ultimate decision-making power most often lies in the hands of delegates who are, frequently, appointed rather than elected. Appointments to the main sporting mega event awarding bodies, FIFA and the IOC, are often made on the basis of political connection or past glory as a participant in a related field, rather than professional-technical expertise in delivering or evaluating major sporting events. Although past scandals have led to a tightening up of the activities of those who ultimately vote in a secret ballot to decide which bidder wins, there is little doubt that decision makers can still base their selection on more subjective criteria (Preuss, 2000). It is little wonder that objective issues such as technical competency take second place when the awarding bodies are cast, by clever candidates, in the role of generous hero with the power to transform lives, enhance communities and (re)build nations.

For prospective candidates, the selection of a bid narrative is not necessarily straightforward. At first glance, it might appear as if there is an established formula to follow. Experienced candidates should follow a reward (or competency) narrative and seek to project a frame to the media and the awarding bodies around possession of existing expertise and excellence. Inexperienced candidates should follow a scholarship narrative and seek to project an emotional message of hope and faith. However, as Preuss (2000) demonstrates, it is important to recognise that bidding decisions are competitive processes which take place in a fluid, complex and contested socio-political and geo-political environment. In effect, those seeking to bid for the most sought after peripatetic events must consider not only their own strengths and weaknesses *vis-à-vis* the formal bid criteria, but also the historic conditions in which the current bid process is being contested, and the relative position, power and intended strategy of their fellow candidates.

Prospective bidders can also obtain competitive advantage by giving consideration to how their bid fits within the wider political environment of the relevant awarding body and a range of contemporary global issues. In Chapter 2 we detailed how major sport event bids have increasingly added new dimensions to the legacy claims and rationales for their bids. Examining bidding narratives, it can be seen that these dimensions are often a means of differentiating a bid from its competitors and addressing, potentially subconscious, concerns within the awarding body relating to wider social concerns of the time. A key example of this is the Rio bid for the 2016 Olympic Games. Despite scoring lower than fellow candidate cities Madrid, Tokyo and Chicago during the technical evaluation (IOC, 2008), Rio's bid proved to be successful in part due to an emotional scholarship narrative which, as mentioned above, highlighted the 'first-time' nature of their hosting. However, it is also worth highlighting the extent to which Rio's bid emphasised an environmental message – 'Green Games for a Blue Planet' (Rio 2016, 2007) – at the heart of its bid. This was reflected not only in the text of the bid book, but also the logo and imagery used throughout the bid campaign. In the face of growing criticism of sporting mega events amongst the general public (Lenskyj, 2008), and awareness of environmental issues across a range of major sporting events such as the Beijing 2008 Summer Olympic Games and Vancouver's 2010 Winter Olympic Games, Rio's sustainability-centred narrative arrived at precisely the right moment to take advantage of a desire for a 'green games'. This added further sustenance to the city's bid and enabled it to overcome technically stronger competitors. Similarly, Los Angeles' bid for the 1984 Olympic Games can be seen, in this light, as a response to concerns regarding spiralling event budgets in the late 1970s. Both Barcelona in 1992 and Sydney in 2000, with their respective focus on culture (Miah & García, 2012) and social and community impacts (IOC, 1993), could be seen as responding to concerns that the Games had become too focussed on economic return. Based on this argument, and reflecting the trends identified in Chapter 2, a bid which offers a response to the social concerns of the day will be better placed than those which focus simply on technical issues or a narrative centred around their internal conditions.

Glasgow 2014: positioning the bid

The example of competitive positioning is best examined by returning to look at Glasgow's ultimately successful bid to host the 2014 Commonwealth Games. Through its bids for events, including the 1990 European Capital of Culture, Glasgow had pursued a strong scholarship narrative. Indeed, so successful was this approach over a thirty-year period, that Mooney (2004) suggested that cities sought to 'do a Glasgow', using the city as a benchmark for event-led regeneration. However, when bidding to host the 2014 Games, Glasgow faced competition from the

Nigerian city of Abuja. Abuja's bid sought to 'complete the circle' (BBC News, 2007) and bring the Games to Africa for the first time, and was predicated on the Games being used to kickstart a massive transformation within the city itself, as well as for the Nigerian nation and wider African continent. When directly compared to Abuja's narrative, a scholarship bid from Glasgow would potentially have lacked credibility. Adoption of a scholarship strategy built on hope and emotion would have appeared naive at best and offensive at worst, when coming from a first world city that played such a significant role as an economic powerhouse at the heart of the British Empire. Whilst the Glasgow bid book did have an element of scholarship in the form of targeted redevelopment of the city's East End (Glasgow, 2014 (2007)), ultimately the bid focussed on aspects of technical competency. Glasgow skilfully positioned its bid as a reward for its incremental, carefully designed sporting, cultural and event investments over the previous thirty years (Stell, 2014). The Games were heralded as the biggest event the city could potentially host, being too small in stature to host a first order sporting mega event, and the city's track record of hosting smaller events of a related nature was repeatedly emphasised (Glasgow, 2014 (2007)) in order to demonstrate the city's capacity and capability. When faced with a competitor who could lay claim to its traditional development narrative, the Glasgow bid moved instead towards a reward narrative and positioned itself as the most capable host city. However, simply demonstrating capability is often not enough to win a bid. Often, as the account above demonstrates, a good scholarship bid will outflank a reward bid as the emotional pull leads to seemingly irrational decisions being taken. Crucially, for Glasgow its bid benefited from the recent history of other Commonwealth Games bids. In 2010, the Games were hosted in India for the first time, as Delhi, which campaigned on a developmental agenda which condensed and crystallised (Baviskar, 2014) the project of making the host a world-class city, acted as host city. However, the lead up to the Games, in Western media at least, was dominated by stories suggesting Delhi was ill-prepared to deliver a successful Games (Mishra, 2012). This concern influenced the bidding process for 2014 which was taking place against this backdrop of unpreparedness. In this situation, Glasgow's reward narrative gained strength and its reputation for delivery of other major events enabled it to be positioned as a 'safe pair of hands' to host the 2014 Games. This safety aspect sat in contrast to another potentially developmental Games in Abuja which, as Kidd (2016) highlights, was identified by the Commonwealth Games Federation's own evaluation panel as potentially lacking in capacity and capability to deliver. Thus, it is clear that hosting candidates must consider not only their own strengths and weaknesses when planning a bid, or indeed only those of their immediate competitors, but also the positioning of their bid in relation to previous bid campaigns for the same event.

Conclusions

In this chapter we have argued that developing a coherent and compelling narrative is imperative to any potential event host. A strong narrative has the ability to underpin a technically sound bid or usurp a competitor bid which is poorly expressed. However, the selection of a winning narrative is a multi-faceted process. Candidates must consider not only their own strengths and weaknesses, but also their relative positioning to competitor bids and the historic context in which their target event and bidding process is located in order to maximise success opportunities. In doing so, and if combined with a technically sound bid process, a powerful momentum can be built by a candidate city. However, as the following chapter demonstrates, these explicit elements of a bid campaign must be married with a more subtle, implicit, lobbying campaign to maximise chances of success.

References

Alegi, P. (2001) 'Feel the pull in your soul': Local agency and global trends in South Africa's 2006 World Cup bid. *Soccer and Society*, 2(3), pp.1–21.

Baviskar, A. (2014) Dreaming big: Spectacular events and the 'world-class' city: The Commonwealth games in Delhi. In J. Grix (ed.), *Leveraging legacies from sports mega-events: Concepts and cases* (pp.130–141), London: Palgrave Macmillan.

BBC News (2003) Why Liverpool won. Available at http://news.bbc.co.uk/1/hi/uk/2962008.stm (accessed 22 December 2016).

BBC News (2007) Abuja 'not troubled' by Glasgow. Available at http://news.bbc.co.uk/1/hi/scotland/glasgow_and_west/6496889.stm (accessed 22 December 2016).

Black, D. (2007) The symbolic politics of sport mega-events: 2010 in comparative perspective. *Politikon*, 34(3), pp.261–276.

Black, D. (2008) Dreaming big: The pursuit of 'second order' games as a strategic response to globalization. *Sport in Society*, 11(4), pp.467–480.

Brannagan, P.M. and Giulianotti, R. (2015) Soft power and soft disempowerment: Qatar, global sport and football's 2022 World Cup finals. *Leisure Studies*, 34(6), pp.703–719.

Brighenti, O., Clivaz, C., Délétroz, N. and Favre, N. (2005) *From initial idea to success: A guide to bidding for sports events for politicians and administrators*. Chavannes-Lausanne, Switzerland: Sports Event Network for Tourism and Economic Development of the Alpine Space.

Connolly, M.G. (2013) The 'Liverpool model(s)': cultural planning, Liverpool and Capital of Culture 2008. *International Journal of Cultural Policy*, 19(2), pp.162–181.

Cornelissen, S. (2004) 'It's Africa's turn!' The narratives and legitimations surrounding the Moroccan and South African bids for the 2006 and 2010 FIFA finals. *Third World Quarterly*, 25(7), pp.1293–1309.

Cornelissen, S. and Swart, K. (2006) The 2010 Football World Cup as a political construct: The challenge of making good on an African promise. *The Sociological Review*, 54(s2), pp.108–123.

Cox, T. and O'Brien, D. (2012) The 'scouse wedding' and other myths: Reflections on the evolution of a 'Liverpool model' for culture-led urban regeneration. *Cultural Trends*, 21(2), pp.93–101.

Dorsey, J.M. (2014) The 2022 World Cup: A potential monkey wrench for change. *The International Journal of the History of Sport*, 31(14), pp.1739–1754.

García, B., Melville, R. and Cox, T. (2010) *Creating an impact: Liverpool's experience as European Capital of Culture*. Impacts 08.

Glasgow 2014 (2007) People, place, passion: Glasgow 2014 Commonwealth Games candidate city file. Available at http://www.thecgf.com/media/games/2014/G2014_CCF_Vol1-3.pdf (accessed 22 December 2016).

Griffiths, E. (2000) *Bidding for glory: Why South Africa lost the Olympic and World Cup bids, and how to win next time.* Johannesburg: Jonathan Ball Publishers.

Grix, J. (2012) 'Image' leveraging and sports mega-events: Germany and the 2006 FIFA World Cup. *Journal of Sport & Tourism,* 17(4), pp.289–312.

Humphreys, B.R. and Prokopowicz, S. (2007) Assessing the impact of sports mega-events in transition economies: EURO 2012 in Poland and Ukraine. *International Journal of Sport Management & Marketing,* 2(5–6), pp.496–509.

International Olympic Committee (1993) *Report IOC Enquiry Commission for the Games of the XXVII Olympiad 2000.* Lausanne: IOC.

International Olympic Committee (2008) *Report of the 2016 IOC Evaluation Commission.* Lausanne: IOC.

Jones, C. (2013) Winning Capital of Culture for Liverpool, by the people who did it. Available at http://www.liverpoolecho.co.uk/news/nostalgia/winning-capital-culture-liverpool-people-4066287 (accessed 22 December 2016).

Kidd, M.A. (2016) *'Expanding horizons': Investigating the Glasgow 2014 legacy for young people in the East End of Glasgow* (Doctoral dissertation, University of Glasgow).

Lenskyj, H.J. (2008) *Olympic industry resistance: Challenging Olympic power and propaganda.* Albany: SUNY Press.

Little, S. (2008) Liverpool '08 – brand and contestation. In L. Malikova and M. Sirak (eds), *Regional and urban regeneration in European peripheries: What role for culture?* (pp.44–50). Bratislava: Institute of Public Policy.

Liverpool Echo (2016) Liverpool set to bid to host 2026 Commonwealth Games. Available at http://www.liverpoolecho.co.uk/news/liverpool-news/liverpool-set-bid-host-2026-111 76825 (accessed 22 December 2016).

Masterman, G. (2009) *Strategic sports event management.* Olympic edn. Amsterdam: Elsevier Butterworth-Heinemann.

McGillivray, D. (2014) Digital cultures, acceleration and mega sporting event narratives. *Leisure Studies,* 33(1), pp.96–109.

Miah, A. and García, B. (2012) *The Olympics: The basics.* London: Routledge.

Mishra, S. (2012) 'The Shame Games': a textual analysis of Western press coverage of the Commonwealth Games in India. *Third World Quarterly,* 33(5), pp.871–886.

Mooney, G. (2004) Cultural policy as urban transformation? Critical reflections on Glasgow, European City of Culture 1990. *Local Economy,* 19(4), pp.327–340.

Peña, E.F., de Moragas, M., Lallana, I. and Rezende, A. (2010) Spain: The power of a mega event which eclipses criticism. *The International Journal of the History of Sport,* 27(9–10), pp.1634–1674.

Platt, L. (2011) Liverpool 08 and the performativity of identity. *Journal of Policy Research in Tourism, Leisure & Events,* 3(1), pp.31–43.

Preuss, H. (2000) Electing an Olympic city – a multidimensional decision. In K.B. Wamsley, S.G. Martyn, G.H. MacDonald and R.K. Barney (eds), *Bridging three centuries: Intellectual crossroads and the modern Olympic movement* (pp.89–104). London: 5th International Symposium for Olympic Research.

Rio 2016 (2007) *Rio 2016: Candidature file for Rio de Janeiro to host the 2016 Olympic and Paralympic Games,* Rio: Rio 2016.

Rojek, C. (2013) *Event power: How global events manage and manipulate.* London: Sage.

Scharfenort, N. (2012) Urban development and social change in Qatar: The Qatar National Vision 2030 and the 2022 FIFA World Cup. *Journal of Arabian Studies,* 2(2), pp.209–230.

Shoval, N. (2002) A new phase in the competition for the Olympic gold: the London and New York bids for the 2012 Games. *Journal of Urban Affairs,* 24(5), pp.583–599.

Stell, M. (2014) Candidate cities, citizens and the Commonwealth Games: The limits of aspiration. In K. Spracklen, S. Dun and N. Wise (eds), *Game changer: The transformative potential of sport* (pp.127–142). Whitney: Inter-Disciplinary Press.

The Guardian (2002) Six cities shortlisted for culture capital bid. Available at https://www.theguardian.com/uk/2002/oct/31/travelnews.travel1 (accessed 22 December 2016).

6

BIDDING TACTICS

Campaigning and lobbying

Introduction

In the first part of this book we set out why cities and nations bid for major events, whether sporting, cultural or commercial. In Chapter 5 we discussed the importance of developing a story; a coherent and convincing narrative that accompanies a bid that can be communicated effectively to awarding bodies and other internal and external audiences. In this chapter, our focus turns to the campaigning tactics employed by bid committees and their support networks when seeking to communicate their agreed narrative to a variety of publics. In doing so, we consider both internal and external publics, emphasising examples of successful campaigns and evaluating their recipes for success. Structurally, we begin by focusing upon the specific tactics utilised by bid committees to enhance their chances of being awarded the major prize they seek, drawing upon a discussion of the Tokyo bid for the 2020 Olympic Games. We then move beyond the operation of a bid campaign and locate the campaigning and lobbying approaches within a broader framework of soft power and cultural diplomacy, as these have become increasingly important macro drivers underpinning event bidding. Finally, we consider the negative consequences of poorly conceived campaigns for bid organisations and the cities/nations they represent.

Bidding campaigns: principles and practices

Firstly, it is necessary to look at the specific tactics used by bid committees and their networks to attract the attention of awarding bodies and domestic and international publics. There are a number of tactics worthy of further scrutiny here: media and PR messaging; candidate city presentations at international conferences; presence at international events and exhibitions; and lobbying visits to awarding body member's location. Whilst we recognise that formal opportunities to interact with voting delegates and other influencers are not the only factors that lead to a successful bid (see Chapter 7 on impropriety and corruption), they are essential forums for bid organisations to communicate their message effectively.

Tokyo 2020: delivery, celebration and innovation

Tokyo's successful bid to host the 2020 Olympic Games illustrates the importance of carefully designed campaigns and lobbying activity. Formally, Tokyo (and its competitors) had four opportunities to present its case to IOC delegates. The lead strategic communications advisor to the 2020 bid, from a UK-based PR agency, emphasised the importance of differentiating Tokyo's bid from the 2016 failed attempt, stressing the need to adopt a "more aggressive, 'Western' style of campaigning" to address a perception that the failed Tokyo 2016 bid had been "technically excellent, but which suffered notably from a perceived lack of passion and excitement" (Varley, 2013 [online]). Learning from failed bids is an important feature of future bidding success, as discussed in Chapter 4. Tokyo utilised its four formal presentation opportunities to present several vital messages. First, at the international SportAccord convention the bid committee emphasised Tokyo's ability to deliver the event as a 'safe pair of hands' for the IOC's main asset. At subsequent presentations the bid committee sought to introduce an element of surprise to their campaign, drawing on personal anecdotes and storytelling techniques, including employing a Paralympian athlete to open the final presentation to IOC delegates. Once the candidate cities were reduced to the final three, they were required to present to voting IOC members and this represented another crucial opportunity to influence wavering voters for the final time. One of the main reasons why Tokyo was awarded the rights to host the 2020 Summer Olympic Games in 2013 was due to the quality of their final presentation in Buenos Aires. In that final presentation they focused on the main three strengths – delivery (the 'safe pair of hands' notion we discussed in Chapters 4 and 5), celebration (Tokyo would provide an outstanding visitor experience during the Games) and innovation (building on the stereotype of Japan as a technologically advanced society). However, crucially, the bid committee's success in countering cultural stereotypes by adopting an informal, emotional and visually powerful approach won out.

Alongside the formal presentations that each candidate city is required to give, the Tokyo bid team also exploited other campaigning and lobbying tactics during the bid cycle to position itself as the competitor to beat. First, it had a strong presence in London during the 2012 Olympic Games as a means of leveraging media coverage, demonstrating their understanding that this city is a central hub where international media outlets are located. Second, they also launched their Candidature File to an international audience in London in early 2013 – again taking advantage of the media hub that exists in that city and exploiting the feel good factor produced by the London 2012 Olympic Games. Exploiting these early opportunities allowed Tokyo to position itself as the most likely host city to be able to deliver the Games as successfully as London had.

Activating the bid brand

Subsequent Olympic candidate cities have also followed the example of Tokyo in exploiting the opportunities presented by collective gatherings of influential stakeholders to intensify their campaigning and lobbying activities. This also reflects an increasing managerialism and professionalism that informs event bids, where 'experts' in finance, marketing, public relations and communications are recruited to ensure the right message is portrayed to the right audiences. For example, during the 2016 Olympic Games in Rio, each of the four candidate cities (at that time) for the 2024 Games (Rome, Paris, Los Angeles and Budapest) brought a significant physical, media and personnel presence to the city. LA 2024 sent its full 25-person team to Brazil to staff an exhibition presence on Ipanema beach and to travel around the city meeting and greeting the 100+ IOC delegates and more than 2,000 representatives of international sporting federations, national Olympic committees and sponsors present during the Games. Drawing on the language of marketing communications, each bid attempted to present its key messages to delegates via face-to-face meetings, attendance at official functions and participation in the IOC's formal observer programme (limited to eight representatives from each candidate city). Candidate cities seek to build on existing relationships and create new ones with the people who will ultimately decide the fate of their bid. To demonstrate the importance of securing support through attraction and persuasion, the LA 2024 bid committee alone had a $75 million campaign budget (Reid, 2016). As Terrence Burns, LA 2024's Chief Marketing Officer has suggested, a press release or one presentation is unlikely to be decisive in influencing an ageing IOC membership with their bid's message of innovation and technology:

> [W]e have 15 or 16 months here to build a communication campaign that will culminate in Lima around (the bid's core points of emphasis). So we're going to have to show them, not tell them, and we have some tactical plans around our communications planning going forward with the bid that I think will be illustrative of what value we can bring to the Olympic movement, to this particular target audience.
>
> *(Reid, 2016 [online])*

Linked to communications is the importance afforded to the appointment of a team of experienced consultants that can be called upon to win the case overseas – people with contacts, networks and influence and, crucially, previous experience of successful bids. This feeds into the communication strategy, and what works in terms of influencing opinion formers and decision makers. As we know, bid committees now invariably spend significant sums of money on communication strategies. For example, in order to rebuff reputational concerns that lingered about China, Beijing's bid committee for the 2008 Olympic Games commissioned two international PR agencies to ensure the key messages coming from the bid team were suitable for European and American audiences in particular (D'Hooghe, 2015). This, D'Hooghe (2015) argues was part of Beijing's proactive public diplomacy through events.

'Backing the bid': generating internal and external support

Another key tactic of bid committees is to demonstrate that they carry sufficient public support to ensure they satisfy the awarding body criteria (see Chapter 4 on technical elements). Again, bid teams use communications and messaging strategies to generate strong domestic support. 'Back the bid' or equivalent campaigns are commonplace – often making it as simple as possible for the public to pledge their support to the bid. Popular politicians, sport stars and other celebrities are also co-opted as bid supporters at this time to maximise positive coverage. Paris, a candidate city for the 2016 Olympic Games co-opted Paul Pogba, an internationally recognisable sport star to help it generate greater public support for its bid. But Paris also sought to utilise contemporary crowdfunding techniques to achieve two separate but interlinked objectives. First, it wanted to raise funds to help minimise public investment in the Games (an increasingly problematic feature of event bids); and, second, it wanted to demonstrate public support. By purchasing wristbands, the public were asked to visibly (and financially) pledge their support. However, this initiative to involve the public failed, with less than 10% of the target (€10 million) achieved a year after its launch. Foley et al. (2012) have shown how a consumerist logic underpinning backing the bid can mask real levels of public support. In response, the Paris 2024 bid committee launched the 'biggest public engagement initiative in Olympic bid history' (Etchells, 2016) designed to involve the general public in shaping the content of the bid document. Cynically, these tactics appear to be about addressing public apathy about sporting mega event bids and gesture politics, as opposed to actually demonstrating a commitment to public involvement in decision making.

The LA 2024 and Paris 2024 examples highlight the importance of clever public relations and communication strategies, but another common tactic employed by bid committees is the involvement of state representatives and institutions in mobilising support from international networks. Reflecting on Rio's successful bid in 2009, Schausteck de Almeida, Marchi Júnior & Pike (2014) highlight how the bid committee communicated its key messages using the conduit of the Brazilian government's Ministry of Foreign Affairs:

> all the Brazilian Embassies during the bid phase were informed about the Olympic bid, instructed to mention it in every public event and supported any Brazilian sport delegation abroad. The diplomats were expected to contact IOC voting members, presidents of international federations and National Olympic Committees, government authorities and sportspeople that could influence the choice of Rio de Janeiro to host the 2016 Games.
>
> *(p.278)*

Beyond the involvement of governmental institutions in influencing decision makers via existing diplomatic mechanisms, political leaders themselves have also played an important role in bidding contests over the years. Three prominent Olympic Games' examples deserve consideration here. First, Tony Blair, the UK Prime Minister when London was awarded the rights to host the 2012 Olympic Games in 2007, was an extremely proactive supporter of the bid from the outset. He, and his Labour Government of the time, viewed the Olympics as an opportunity to extend the Cool Britannia brand that they had sought to exploit (Rojek, 2013). He also travelled to Singapore for the final IOC vote and lobbied strongly for London's right to host the event. In contrast, after Chicago's failed bid for the 2016 Olympic Games, President Obama was subjected to criticism for his relatively late appearance, only becoming a high profile advocate for the bid in the last week of the campaign when the city's Mayor and other civic leaders convinced him that his appearance would sway a close vote. The Chicago bid team had expected Obama's international 'star' appeal to help them over the line at the final event in Copenhagen in 2009 but they were, instead, eliminated in the first round of voting. In comparison, Brazil's President Lula was very proactive in his desire to be 'seen' to be wholly behind the Rio 2016 bid from early on, culminating in his attendance at the vote in Copenhagen in 2009 which had been trailed for some time. He spoke as a representative of a country that was experiencing exceptional economic growth and making an impression in international affairs.

The role of celebrity endorsements and ambassadors should also not be underestimated. Talking about both global humanitarian events and sporting mega events, Rojek (2013) suggests that they "rely upon a celebrity to humanise event management campaigns" (p.29) and "by drawing in 'representative' superstars from film, television, pop music and sport, events apply an emulsive lick of glamour and star power to the event process" (p.54). Over the last few event cycles, ambassadors for Olympic Games and FIFA World Cup bids have included Jackie Chan (Beijing, 2008 Olympic Games), David Beckham (London, 2012 Olympic Games), Muhammed Ali (New York, 2012 Olympic Games bid), Franz Beckenbauer and Boris Becker (Germany, 2006 FIFA World Cup). However, whilst there may be a benefit in terms of attracting interest for a bid campaign, there are also dangers associated with the use of celebrities or famous people, because celebrity advocacy can be unstable and weak, at risk of "being deemed inauthentic, because the celebrity advocates themselves are questioned thus" (Brockington, 2014:89). This fear of inauthenticity or questions over motive do not seem to deter bid committees, and it is now commonplace for celebrity ambassadors, particularly those famous for their sporting achievements, to add a degree of glamour to bidding campaigns. Bid committees, run like PR agencies, now exploit every opportunity afforded to them to influence and curry favour with decision makers, albeit they have to be careful to stay within the rules of the Games laid down by the IOC (see Chapter 7 for examples of high profile impropriety).

South Africa 2006: the politics of lobbying

Griffiths (2000) highlights the importance played by senior political figures in his book *Bidding for glory*, which provides a detailed account of South Africa's unsuccessful bid for the 2006 FIFA World Cup, eventually won by Germany. In this account, Griffiths accentuates the importance of senior level dialogue and deal-making to ensure blocks of votes are delivered to bid cities in advance of the official vote at the IOC Congress. Evidence he generated from involvement in the South Africa 2006 bid as a media consultant for the bid team was that they struggled to recover from a perception that African support was split because of Morocco's bid, meaning that there were difficulties encountered in securing the backing of the Asian Confederation, for example. As Griffiths (2000) stresses, Danny Jordaan CEO of the South Africa 2006 bid fought the campaign on two fronts – a strong technical submission (bid document and inspection) and coordinated lobbying activities. The latter involved coordinated visits and presentations to the 24 FIFA Executive Committee members in their own countries alongside a visible bid presence at high profile international events and exhibitions, as well as harnessing political support from Nelson Mandela and Govan Mbeki who interacted with their counterparts in key territories where votes were not assured. For example, it was deemed essential for Mandela to write letters of greeting to both the "King of Saudi Arabia and the Emir of Qatar since it was clear that the FIFA Executive Members from both these countries would be heavily influenced by the views of their governments" (Griffiths, 2000:105). No opportunity for political glad-handing could be missed, and public event opportunities to promote the bid were manufactured regularly, especially when they provided an opportunity to meet face-to-face target voters. However, what bid committees realise is that:

> in truth, such formal presentations amounted to not much more than a charade. The reality is that FIFA Executive Committee members are guided more by political considerations and loyalty to the interests of the confederation than by the quality of stadia and telecommunications systems.
>
> *(p. 108)*

Whilst elsewhere we have considered the importance of technical competency as a determinant of bid success, there is also an important political element to the technical inspection visits to potential host cities that are part of campaign tactics. In the case of the FIFA World Cup, this necessitates numerous presentations and rounds of questioning on the readiness of venues, transport infrastructure, security, and the state of the economy, amongst other criteria. However, the way the visit is managed and the impression that Executive Committee members are left with of the potential host is almost as important as technical competency. Griffiths (2000) again details the case of South Africa (2006) when the technical inspection team was exposed to eight government minister presentations, fine dining, stadium visits and high quality hospitality, shattering "the impression of SAFA as inefficient and disorganized" (Griffiths, 2000:121). Conventional wisdom suggests that hosts need to secure a balance between technical proficiency, organisational efficiency and a sprinkling of shock and awe, whether in the form of powerful speeches from leaders, surprise appearances from celebrity ambassadors or 'authentic' heart-warming stories from the most marginal or powerless in the society. For South Africa 2006, Nelson Mandela met with each member of the FIFA technical inspection team with words for their respective heads of state, and each received a personal photograph with the President (Griffiths, 2000).

However, what is also noticeable about the bid campaigns for all major sporting events is that, despite a range of campaigning and lobbying tactics being employed, it is rare for a candidate to be assured of victory in advance of the final presentation and vote. Because the voting is invariably politically motivated, support can shift and promises can be broken. Commitments and guarantees are worth little until the final voting takes place, via a secret ballot. In several high profile cases, the favourite has lost because of last minute promises or inducements that have led some delegates to switch their vote. Bid teams often call upon the highest level of diplomacy and influence available to reduce the likelihood of such an eventuality playing out, but even President Nelson Mandela could do little to prevent the New Zealand Executive Committee member abstaining on the second vote for the 2006 FIFA World Cup, handing the victory to Germany as a result. Sometimes, blocks of votes (e.g. South America or Africa) are secured on the basis of informal agreement about reciprocal future support, whilst on others formal agreements are signed to 'guarantee' these same agreements. Of course, like all political elections, agreements made in good faith at the time may not necessarily come to fruition in the future, because of a change of leadership in the awarding body (e.g. Sepp Blatter's resignation from FIFA), for example.

Major events, soft power and bidding

As we outlined in the first part of this book, international events are increasingly important within a globalising world, reflecting the growing levels of inter-connectedness and social consciousness of the world as a single place (Brannagan & Giulianotti, 2014). Sporting mega events and cultural events also have an increased political saliency to a wide variety of governmental and non-governmental actors across the world. International expos and sporting mega events, in particular, have historically been used by political elites to project their nation's assets (economic and cultural) to international audiences, but the instrumental use of major events to achieve non-sporting or cultural goals has intensified and accelerated over the last thirty years. The way international event bids are planned and organised is variegated, nations can "adapt, innovate and manoeuvre...to differentiate themselves from each other" (Brannagan & Giulianotti, 2014:3). Bidding to host sporting mega events, for example, is used instrumentally to create new 'brand' identities (for host and global audiences), bring about change in international image and reputation or achieve domestic or foreign policy objectives (Grix & Houlihan, 2014). Oft-cited examples include the way Germany used the 2006 FIFA World Cup to project a new, open, friendly image that has continued to reap rewards in the years since, economically and politically. In its bid campaign, South Africa portrayed its hosting of the 2010 FIFA World Cup as a reward for the entire African continent – as a symbol of unity, solidarity and peace (Cornelissen, 2004). Furthermore, host cities and nations also view bidding for sporting and cultural events as effective ways to enter the world stage and to "symbolically challenge the traditional global order" (Schausteck de Almeida et al., 2014:272). In Chapter 3 we discussed the rationales underpinning bids for sporting and cultural events as significant elements of a globalised politics, influencing and being influenced by politics and foreign policy (Jackson & Haigh, 2008). Having demonstrated how lobbying works within bid campaigns, our attention now turns to demonstrating how bidding campaigns can contribute to wider political agendas within the prospective host nation.

International events are inseparable from politics, international relations and diplomacy (whether public or cultural). They are also now accepted as an important element in nations' soft power (Nye, 2004) offensives, to the point that securing a positive impact on the nation's image (or brand) or international prestige has moved from being a welcome consequence to a significant justification for bidding for, and winning, the rights to host mega sports events (Grix & Houlihan, 2014). Soft power relates to the "the ability to get what you want through attraction rather than coercion or payments" (Nye, 2004:256) or "power achieved when people, institutions or nation states accept the authority of others as normal by way of culture, politics or policies" (Schausteck de Almeida et al., 2014: 273). In particular, for those nations that do not possess (or are unwilling to deploy) hard power leverage (military force or economic resources), major sporting or cultural events are thought to provide a valuable strategic vehicle to generate influence in the world or simply as a charm offensive to attract the interest of desired audiences. Drawing on the example of Qatar's successful bid for the 2022 FIFA World Cup, Brannagan & Giulianotti (2014) argue that "core concepts and images emerge here, of competence, professionalism, technological sophistication and international benevolence, as the basis for Qatar's soft power strategy" (p.8). The Qatar FIFA World Cup bid, including the campaigning and lobbying tactics employed, cannot be separated from the more general international engagement strategy underway in that territory. This small state had already taken steps to be a more influential partner in international security, global social issues and peace building, prior to its eventual bid for the FIFA World Cup. Whilst it can be tempting to view event bids in a vacuum, as isolated 'happenings' in their own right, it is more realistic to see them as tactical outcomes of broader soft power strategies. South Africa's bids for the Olympic Games in 2004 (Cape Town, unsuccessful), the FIFA World Cup (2006, unsuccessful) and again in 2010 (successful) further reinforces the long game that potential hosts are participating in. South Africa was able to employ a 'deserving' narrative for their 2010 bid after having lost out by the smallest of margins in 2006.

London certainly used its bid for the 2012 Olympic Games as a means of extending its soft power offensive and re-imagining Britain's place in the world order after a few decades of declining influence. As Grix & Houlihan (2014) have suggested, the use of a sport event in this way was a departure for the British political elites, as sport had not been a principal feature of public diplomacy up until that point. However, in both the bid, and subsequent planning and delivery, the Foreign and Commonwealth Office played a significant role in using the opportunity presented by the Games to enhance the UK's reputation overseas. Thematically, they promoted British culture, the UK economy and the enhancement of security by harnessing Olympic values (Grix & Houlihan, 2014). Soft power offensives can also be directed at the awarding bodies, as opposed to other potential actors. So, Schausteck de Almeida et al. (2014:272) argue that bid teams often try to "identify themselves as representatives of wider emerging territories or cultures" as a means of meeting the awarding bodies' stated desire to take their event assets to new locations as part of a development, diversity or equality agenda. Rio's successful bid for the 2016 Olympic Games was based on projecting its status as a rising economic and political power, influencing international developments. It was also making an emotional appeal on behalf of the entire South American continent, which had, until then, failed to host an Olympic Games. In its presentations to the IOC, the Rio bid team regularly showed maps of the world where the modern Olympic Games had been held, in order to graphically illustrate the omission of South America – a shrewd tactic designed to both appeal to the developmental agenda of the IOC and to, by definition, draw attention to the relative bounty of awards that other parts of the world have enjoyed.

Soft disempowerment: the loser's curse

Of course, bidding for sporting mega events can also produce negative consequences, politically, economically and socially for host destinations. Brannagan & Giulianotti (2014) have coined the term 'soft disempowerment' to explain the potentially deleterious reputational damage that can arise when a nation fails to deliver a successful sporting mega event, or draws attention to its failings when greater media exposure is brought upon it (during bidding or on successful award). However, poorly organised bid campaigns using the wrong tactics can also lead to a litany of negative aftershocks. In Chapter 4 we highlighted how Aberdeen's failure to be shortlisted for the 2017 UK Capital of Culture led to a well-publicised fall out about poor organisation, lack of vision, and the like, summed up by the headline 'Hang your heads in shame over city of culture failure' (*Press and Journal*, 2013). In the sporting mega event world, the tremors are much more profound when a bid fails and the focus turns to the reasons why. As previously mentioned, Chicago failed to effectively manage the diplomacy required to secure the necessary votes for the 2016 Olympic Games. Bid campaigns, when unsuccessful, have financial and political costs. Budgets, often bolstered by public subsidy (Lauermann, 2016), are scrutinised, the proposed benefits of bidding are subjected to media attention and the future prospects of the city or nation on the global stage are open to conjecture. When failing to win the rights to host the 2012 Olympic Games, Paris was so embarrassed that it said it was unlikely to bid again. Similarly, when Egypt failed in its attempt to be the host for the African continent's FIFA World Cup in 2010, the aftermath drew attention to political and financial corruption in the nation and in its football federation.

And yet, despite the potentially negative consequences internally and externally in terms of international reputation, many cities and nations do try again. They do go through the long and laborious process of announcing their candidacy and initiate ambitious urban development masterplans and the like. As discussed, South Africa failed to win the Olympic Games in 2004 and the FIFA World Cup in 2006, but that did not stop them from bidding and winning the rights to hold the FIFA World Cup in 2010. In terms of campaigning and lobbying tactics, South Africa learned from previous experiences, exploiting the perceived injustice of their previous failed bids to eventually triumph; although this award is tainted by accusations of bribery that hang over a number of recent FIFA World Cup bid processes (*The Guardian*, 2015). Pyeongchang, in South Korea, eventually won the rights to host the 2018 Winter Olympic Games after having bid unsuccessfully on two previous occasions. Toronto lost the race to be the 2008 host, against a tide of negativity in Canada since the debt problems associated with the Montreal Olympic Games, but the nation subsequently won the right to host the 2010 Winter Olympic Games, this time in Vancouver. As discussed in Chapter 4, there is a fine line to be trodden by prospective host cities and nations between bidding in order to be seen (alibi bids) without a realistic chance of success and being accused of serial bidding which can damage a host's reputation.

Conclusion

Bid committees differ in their constitution, mode of operation and governance, but they all share one common goal – to secure the rights to host a peripatetic event for their city or nation. The stakes are high, the competition is intense, and there is inevitably only one winner. Bid committees and their governmental and private sector sponsors make extravagant promises to improve their chances of being awarded first prize in the bidding contests they enter, but they also employ a range of more subtle, marketing-informed strategies and tactics to persuade awarding bodies that they are the best candidate. In this chapter, we have demonstrated how marketing and public relations techniques are increasingly influential in the campaigning and lobbying tactics employed by bid organisations. Consultants with intellectual capital from previous bids or with experience of international diplomacy are commissioned to design campaigns that win the hearts and minds of decision makers within the awarding bodies. Political support is crucial, as public diplomacy activities are executed to help persuade sporting federations and the awarding body that a city or nation's bid is the one that will best showcase their event asset. We have detailed how effective winning bids have been at navigating the technical and political machinations that accompany each and every sporting mega event bidding process, in particular. Yet, not everyone can be a winner and there are negative reputational, political and economic outcomes from bidding processes that arise as a result of poorly coordinated or managed bid campaigns and ineffective lobbying. Finally, discussed in more detail in Chapter 8, not all campaign tactics and lobbying techniques are legitimate, either within the law or the rules of the game set out by awarding bodies. The high stakes involved in bidding for a sporting mega event, in particular, lead bid committees to either circumnavigate or tread a fine line between the legal and ethical frameworks in place to ensure they give themselves the best chance of success. Event bidding is a political act and the content of bidding documentation can be used to advance some actors' political ambitions.

References

Brannagan, P.M. and Giulianotti, R. (2014) Soft power and soft disempowerment: Qatar, global sport and football's 2022 World Cup finals. *Leisure Studies*, 34(6), pp.703–719.

Brockington, D. (2014) The production and construction of celebrity advocacy in international development. *Third World Quarterly*, 35(1), pp.88–108.

Cornelissen, S. (2004) Sport mega-events in Africa: Processes, impacts and prospects. *Tourism and Hospitality Planning and Development*, 1(1), pp.39–55.

D'Hooghe, I. (2015) *China's public diplomacy*. Leiden: Brills Nijhoff.

Etchells, D. (2016) Paris 2024 to launch 'biggest public engagement initiative in Olympic bid history'. Available at http://www.insidethegames.biz/articles/1036112/paris-2024-to-launch-biggest-public-engagement-initiative-in-olympic-bid-history (accessed 26 August 2016).

Foley, M., McGillivray, D. and McPherson, G. (2012) *Event policy: From theory to strategy*. London: Routledge.

Griffiths, E. (2000) *Bidding for glory: Why South Africa lost the Olympic and World Cup bids and how to win next time*. Johannesburg: Jonathan Ball Publishers.

Grix, J. and Houlihan, B. (2014) Sports mega-events as part of a nation's soft power strategy: The cases of Germany (2006) and the UK (2012). *The British Journal of Politics and International Relations*, 16(4), pp.572–596.

Jackson, S.J. and Haigh, S. (2008) Between and beyond politics: Sport and foreign policy in a globalizing world. *Sport in Society*, 11(4), pp.349–358.

Lauermann, J. (2016) Boston's Olympic bid and the evolving urban politics of event-led development. *Urban Geographies*, 37(2), pp.313–321.

Nye, J.S. (2004) *Soft power: The means to success in world politics*. Cambridge, MA: PublicAffairs.

Press and Journal (2013) Hang your heads in shame over city of culture failure. Available at http://www.pressreader.com/uk/the-press-and-journal-aberdeen/20130620/281479273982628 (accessed 19 August 2016).

Reid, S. (2016) LA2014 gears up for its Olympic campaign season, The Orange County Register. Available at http://www.ocregister.com/articles/olympic-723462-bid-games.html (accessed 18 August 2016).

Rojek, C. (2013) *Event power: How global events manage and manipulate*. London: Sage.

Schausteck de Almeida, B., Marchi Júnior, W. and Pike, E. (2014) The 2016 Olympic and Paralympic Games and Brazil's soft power. *Contemporary Social Science: Journal of the Academy of Social Sciences*, 9(2), pp.271–283.

The Guardian (2015) Fifa crisis: South Africa denies paying $10m bribe for 2010 World Cup. Available at https://www.theguardian.com/football/2015/jun/01/fifa-danny-jordaan-south-africa-no-bribe-2010-world-cup (accessed 17 August 2016).

Varley, N. (2013) How a London agency helped Tokyo's Olympic bid strike gold. *The Drum*. Available at http://www.thedrum.com/opinion/2013/09/13/how-london-agency-helped-tokyos-olympic-bid-strike-gold (accessed 17 August 2016).

PART III

Resistance: corruption and contestation

7

GOVERNANCE, ETHICS AND IMPROPRIETY

Introduction

Over recent years, the environment for event bidding has been subject to intense scrutiny, both politically and in terms of broader public reaction. Numerous scandals have engulfed the main international peripatetic event bidding processes and increased the scrutiny on these global mega-spectacles. In this chapter, we focus primarily on the bidding processes for major sporting events, though there will also be clear implications for other bidding processes, including for cultural and commercial events. Structurally, we begin by setting out the importance of global sports organisations (GSOs) and their status as supranational bodies with the concomitant exemptions they enjoy from national, and at times international, financial and legal restrictions by way of their particular history and constitution. Second, we discuss governance processes from the perspective of the event bidding bodies themselves. Within this discussion we draw attention to the politics of the bidding process, including how the voting process operates for the most sought after major events. Finally, we focus on the challenges to governance and accountability facing major sports events and consider what these mean for the future of peripatetic events; will they simply tighten up their processes due to the pressure to change from external publics and internal sponsors and continue to flourish or is there a real dubiety as to whether there their core 'asset', the mega event itself, is damaged beyond repair?

Sport events and GSOs: territoriality, jurisdiction and non-profits

As discussed in previous chapters, the main peripatetic events that attract bidding attention are the FIFA World Cup and the Olympic Games (Summer and Winter versions). Whilst there has been a proliferation of awarding bodies created to manage the bidding process for other events (e.g. European Capital of Culture and the World Expo), it is the awarding process for the two largest sporting events that have been the subject of the most scrutiny in the media over accountability, transparency and potential impropriety. Before focusing on specific examples of event bidding processes that have come under attack, it is necessary to provide a brief historical account of the origins of the global sport organisations that 'own' the world's largest sport events – the FIFA World Cup and Olympic Games – to provide an insight into how they have become so (all) powerful.

Forster (2016) plots the emergence and development of GSOs to the nineteenth century and the more generalised professionalisation of sport. Whereas sport had been viewed as an amateur and largely ungoverned activity in previous eras, from the nineteenth century onwards it was formalised, subject to structured rules and opened up to commercialisation processes. GSOs initially "set the framework and policies that allow sport to operate at a global level" (Forster, 2016:2) but as the years went on, they became much more involved in the "invention, ownership and control of global sports events such as World Championships and the Olympic Games" (ibid.), benefitting from the revenues that these events produced. Whilst the main GSOs, including FIFA and the IOC, continued to operate as non-profit making organisations, they became more successful and attracted larger numbers of members, becoming more powerful globally as a result. As Eick (2010) suggests, FIFA started out as "a kind of Old Boys Network" (p.283) before developing into "a modern profit-oriented and de facto profit-making nonprofit corporation" (ibid.). He argues that as it grew, FIFA's organisational structure formalised and it started to resemble a multinational corporation in terms of management structure.

Not only did the emergence and growth of GSOs lead to increased power and influence over the shape and direction of modern sport *per se*, they also made it difficult for alternative sport bodies to arise. As they attracted more members from across the world, the most prominent GSOs were able to use this power to dictate the rules of the game of modern sport, literally. As Meier & García (2015) suggest, FIFA "attributes to itself the powers to govern and regulate world football in collaboration with continental confederations and national football associations" (p.890). Meier & García argue that the attribution of powers to govern and regulate laid the foundations for the corruption crises of the contemporary period as these 'private' institutions were able to successfully enforce their rules on 'public' authorities, including the state apparatus. As our concern in this text is with event bidding processes rather than the governance of sport overall, it is necessary to illustrate how issues of (extra)territoriality and jurisdiction enable these GSOs to exert such profound influence on the economic, political and cultural fabric of the states they interact with.

Forster (2016) argues that GSOs have "almost trans-national quasi-legal jurisdiction that limits access to the law courts and legal rights of bodies and individuals in their national jurisdictions" (p.2). In other words, these private, non-profit organisations can operate within their own rules and limit the role of the state as a result. One of the best examples of this in action is the way in which, during a sporting mega event, the GSO (e.g. FIFA or the IOC) imposes its own private laws upon the state, via the bid requirements, as discussed in Chapter 4, whereby:

> FIFA forces all applicants for hosting the World Cup (nation-states as well as respective host cities) to accept all branding conditions, commercialization interests and security demands laid down in the so-called FIFA Regulations even before the applicants would know whether they will be allowed to host the World Cup.
>
> *(Eick, 2010:285)*

GSOs, which own the principal sporting mega events, are able to dictate terms to governments before they even apply to become a temporary host of their event asset. Participating in the event bidding process commits prospective hosts to willingly accept the conditions set out by the GSO for the delivery of their event, including their branding, commercialisation and security demands. According to Meier & García (2015), the FIFA World Cup is a major fundraiser for FIFA, enabling it to strengthen its powers in regulation, rule making and as a subsidiser for national football associations. FIFA is able to exploit the commercial value of the FIFA World Cup and engage in transnational private regulation (TPR), which Meier & García (2015) define as "the ability of non-state actors to cooperate across borders in order to establish rules and standards of behaviour in a distinct issue area accepted as legitimate by agents not involved in the rule definition" (p.892). In being able to create and regulate international football competitions, FIFA secured an early advantage, which it has subsequently exploited, to profit from the FIFA World Cup and use these revenues to support more member associations. As others have suggested, FIFA created a financial dependency within small member associations and those from developing football nations, which has benefitted the power of the FIFA executive and the governing body itself (Tomlinson, 2000; Meier & García, 2015). The IOC has, to a lesser extent, been able to exert influence over governments and host cities in terms of their event power (Rojek, 2013), although it is much more reliant on the Olympic Games than the other commercial powers that FIFA has at its disposal. For both, they take great care to defend their autonomy against the pressures of international law and, even when subject to significant contestation of their power, they have (to date) successfully resisted major reform of their nineteenth-century institutions. They are both in effect, stateless, lodging in Switzerland, which enables then to avoid being constrained by the same fiscal and legal structures found in many other nations. Despite both the IOC and FIFA being embroiled in several recent corruption scandals, they have remained remarkably resistant to fundamental changes in their governance structures. So, although the IOC was forced to initiate a number of institutional changes after the Salt Lake City corruption scandal "these changes did not affect the IOC's demand for regulatory autonomy, revenue maximization and control of the IOC's commercial assets" (Meier & García, 2015:903). Similarly, though FIFA has been under even more significant pressure to reform in recent years, Meier &

García (2015) think it is unlikely that FIFA will waive its regulatory powers over governments and football associations as these provide lucrative financial rewards for the organisation.

Global sports organisations, event bidding and corruption

GSOs have extensive power and influence that is difficult to check due to their unique governance structures and legal status. They seem, to many, to operate above the law, able to impose rules and regulations upon local and national states that would be impossible for any other type of public or private entity. They have been subject to criticism from activists, elements of the media, and unsuccessful bidders for decades, but still they continue to attract intense competition to host their major sport event assets, at great cost to public and private investors alike.

FIFA's fiefdom: corruption and improper conduct

Take the case of FIFA. Misconduct and corruption within FIFA have long been denounced (Jennings, 2007; Calvert & Blake, 2014) and there have been numerous calls to increase that organisation's accountability towards stakeholders and public authorities. However, in the last two decades the extent of malpractice, corruption and improper conduct has cast a shadow over the world's foremost global sporting events, in particular. Much of the recent focus on corruption has emerged from the decision of FIFA to award the 2022 FIFA World Cup tournament to the small, oil rich Gulf state of Qatar. The politics behind this decision have been shrouded in mystery since the announcement in 2010, with claims of bribery, vote rigging and concerns about human rights and climate dominating the ensuing years. Sport has been a major soft power tool for Qatar (Brannagan & Giulianotti, 2015). It has invested heavily in attracting sport events to enhance its profile on the international stage. For that reason it was unsurprising that it was willing to throw significant resources at trying to secure the rights to hold the second largest sporting event in the world.

The outcome of the 2022 bidding contest simply reinforced, in the mind of FIFA critics, that the organisation and its bidding processes were deeply flawed and open to claims of systematic corruption. That a wealthy oil rich state, with little football history, can successfully win the rights to host the FIFA World Cup, focused the world's attention on the importance accorded to financial power over the much vaunted social and development rhetoric emanating from the governing body. The extent of corruption present within FIFA came to light in 2010 when the UK newspaper, the *Sunday Times*, recorded influential Confederation Presidents admitting to being offered significant financial sweeteners by bid nations to secure their support (meaning to gain their vote) in the 2018 contest. Whilst FIFA responded with some relatively minor censures, including fines for the Executive Committee members involved, it soon became clear that these corruption accusations were simply the tip of a very large iceberg. Later in 2010, FIFA announced that Russia would host the FIFA World Cup in 2018 and Qatar in 2022. Almost immediately, a number of accusations of impropriety were made by media organisations, competing bid nations and the Swiss authorities, in whose jurisdiction FIFA resides. As early as February 2011, FIFA confirmed that there had been collusion between the Qatar and Spain-Portugal bid teams to trade votes for the 2018 and 2022 contests, and throughout 2011 pressure intensified on the organisation to reform in order to enhance accountability and transparency in its decision making.

Since the sheer scale of accusations about corruption in FIFA came to the world's attention in 2010, the bid processes for Germany (2006), South Africa (2010), Brazil (2014), Russia (2018) and Qatar (2022) have been subject to scrutiny as part of various investigations, some initiated by FIFA and others by external authorities, which started in 2012 when Michael Garcia, an American lawyer, was employed to investigate corruption in world football, which included the 2018 and 2022 bid processes. When his report was eventually delivered in September 2014, FIFA blocked its full publication, instead publishing a 42-page summary which cleared Russia and Qatar of any wrongdoing in respect of the bid contests for the 2018 and 2022 FIFA World Cup, respectively. Garcia resigned in protest at what he claimed were erroneous representations of the facts and conclusions. Whilst FIFA had no doubt hoped this conclusion would have brought to an end accusations of corruption over the awarding of the 2018 and 2022 FIFA World Cups, the Garcia saga was actually just the start of the downfall of some of its most senior figures – most notably its President Sepp Blatter. In May 2015, six FIFA Executive Committee members were arrested and charged with offences related to fraud, racketeering and money laundering relating to the FIFA World Cup bids and other commercial matters. This investigation was initiated by US authorities as part of a worldwide probe into corruption at FIFA. Blatter was eventually required to resign in the summer of 2015 as his position came under intense scrutiny.

The removal of Blatter, the long-standing FIFA President, and several other influential FIFA Executive Committee Members, threw the organisation into turmoil but, crucially, has yet to lead to any of the events already awarded being removed as a result of proven corruption in the bidding process. And yet, as a GSO, FIFA has been forced over the course of the last five years to account for its behaviour within the sphere of international law, whereby its Executive Committee members have been subject to Swiss and American legal processes, which suggest that these organisations' cherished positions are now under threat. That said, the reforms that the new President, Gianni Infantino, has introduced since his election early in 2016 are also under threat as his position is also subject to scrutiny on the basis of financial matters.

Bid corruption and the Olympic Games

The accusations of systematic corruption levelled at FIFA also apply to the IOC, and perhaps for an even longer period of time. As Lenskyj (2000) has described in some detail, since at least the late 1960s the Olympic movement (what she calls the Olympic Industry) has been subject to accusations of bribery and corruption, which came to the public's attention most noticeably in 1998 when details of gift exchanges and services between bid committees and IOC members were published. For Lenskyj (2000) the structure of the IOC in the early 1980s, under the tutelage of Juan Antonio Samaranch, led to the scandals that rocked the institution in the late 1990s. IOC members represented their countries rather than their host National Olympic Committee and were encouraged to visit prospective host cities as guests of bid committees, leading to abuses of their position documented most famously as part of the investigation into Salt Lake City in 1998. As Lenskyj (2000) concludes "bid committees in most cities continued to judge the various arrangements to influence IOC members' votes by Olympic family standards rather than by criteria based on ethical business practices or international antibribery agreements" (p.6). Whilst many Olympic critics presume that explicit bribery took place before the Games became popular again after the success of the Los Angeles 1984 Olympic Games, it was the damning evidence presented through the mass media of excessive gift making (scholarships to family members of IOC delegates), services and hospitality above and beyond the existing 'rules' governing the bid process that preoccupied the IOC and those interested in the Olympics from the late 1990s. Lenskyj argues that the Olympics were (re)politicised at this point, as they became subject to investigations from a range of state and non-state agencies. It also became clear during this period that IOC members were less accountable than bid committees to breaches of the bidding rules, but the activities of Swiss IOC member Marc Hodler in drawing attention to the systemic bribery and corruption taking place eventually led to the IOC having to reform the bid process.

The Salt Lake City bid process corruption scandal highlighted what Lenskyj (2000) has termed "a complex system of relationships among bid committees in the United States, Canada, and Australia, and links between members of bid committees and the IOC" (p.19). Whilst the numerous investigations, resignations and criminal proceedings that followed demonstrate that, ultimately, the Olympic movement is not above the law, the fact that information about these practices only came to the public's attention many years after the bids were decided also highlights an ongoing 'fear' of speaking out against the powerful GSO. The fact that the excessive gift making, service and hospitality afforded to IOC members during bids for Atlanta (1996), Salt Lake City (2002) and, to a lesser extent Sydney (2000) was possible, highlights ethical problems at the heart of the awarding organisation and within the bid committees, even if some of the practices were not deemed illegal at that time. In fact, what the various enquiries and investigations into bid contests from 1996 to 2000 highlight is how commonplace inducements were and the degree of expectation that accompanied IOC member visits to prospective bid cities. Unwritten IOC protocol meant that those hoping to curry favour with IOC members felt almost obliged to provide first-class hospitality and related support to these individuals, their families and, often, to their nation's sport development programmes. Whereas excessive gifts, hospitality and services would be viewed as evidence of bribery in other business or public sector contracting arrangements, within the cosy Olympic family these behaviours were viewed as par for the course when the prize was so great.

What the FIFA and IOC examples confirm is that in terms of the bid processes for the GSOs' main assets, bidders have been able to influence the awarding process, negatively affecting the credibility of the organisations and the competition in the minds of the general public. Because these bids are being made for what bidders hope will be a lucrative prize, the stakes are higher and this also leads to a lack of accountability and transparency in the host bid process.

The host city perspective: governance and event bids

One of the key features of event bidding, when considered under the guise of accountability, transparency and ethics, is the role of the host city or nation bid committee. So, whilst we have argued here that supranational organisations have been able to avoid legal challenge because of their ability to carefully navigate jurisdiction and territory, from the host perspective there is evidence of similar attempts to evade democratic accountability, especially at the early stages of a bid. This works on a number of levels, including the legal status of the bid committee, the reporting lines to democratically accountable bodies and the role of the media as core 'partners' in the bid process.

First, it is important to build on our discussions in Chapter 4 which emphasised that the bid committees formed for major sporting and cultural events are invariably the result of what others have termed 'growth coalitions' between the local (entrepreneurial) state and private business interests (Waitt, 2001). These growth coalitions often come together to initiate the idea of bidding for a particular event, sometimes more than a decade in advance and with the objective to pool public and private investments to most effectively pull together a bid for an event. Bid committees are then, on the surface at least, about partnership – between the local state, the private sector, citizens and the media. As Blakeley (2010) has written, with reference to bids by Barcelona and Manchester for the Olympic Games, partnerships between economic agents and public policy making come together more easily when there is a flagship project to provide a focus. She goes on to suggest that, "Although Manchester's two Olympic bids were unsuccessful, the bid process strengthened partnership-working" (p.133). The need to attract private investment to assuage concerns that the public will pay for an Olympic Games, FIFA World Cup or other sporting event means that the local (and national) business community are, as a matter of course, involved from the outset in bidding processes. Again, as Paton, Mooney & McKee (2012) suggest, "sporting events have a major role in the neo-liberal urban governance seen in the augmentation of partnership and coalitions of growth" (p.1479). However, the purpose of event bidding in a system of neo-liberal urban governance is problematic, for a number of reasons. Lauermann (2016) uses the recent example of Boston's failed bid to host the 2024 Olympic Games to highlight how bid committees, or "mega event planning committees" (p.314) benefit from under-estimated public subsidies to enable them to operate. He argues that we need to know more about what indirect public subsidies are committed to covering cost overruns and delays, incentives to enable sponsors to operate without restrictions and "build legal and financial bridges from bids to other ongoing real estate ventures" (p.316). In particular, Lauermann (2016) expresses concern that, in event bidding contests, "questions remain about the long-term costs of public risk-taking in speculative projects like the Games, and about the motives of bidders who seek to downplay their dependence on public support" (p.316). Drawing on Boston's failed bid for the 2024 Olympic Games, Lauermann highlights how the original bid was built on the notion that no public taxes were required to support the budget. However, because of the renewed interests, and influence, of anti-Olympic movements, the bid ultimately failed when:

> The bid corporation was later engulfed in scandal when activists uncovered an unredacted version of the bid (used for internal negotiations) which promised the use of public funds through tax increment financing for the projects...this scandal launched a broader debate over the city's fiscal priorities, and the bid ultimately ended.
>
> *(p.317)*

The fact that the bid committee tried to divert attention away from potential public subsidy and to focus attention on the positive narrative of the bid as requiring little public investment is also mirrored in debates about the FIFA World Cup. For example, Preuss & Schnitzer (2015) have recently argued that local organising committee budget forecasts in the bidding stages of a FIFA World Cup are deliberately under-estimated to give the impression that profits from the event will be greater. Similarly, Shaw (2008) draws attention to the operations of bid committees and the arrangements they enter into with private sector investors and the state that ultimately commit the state to putting in place exceptional planning legislation if the bid is successful. He suggests that "Olympic bids...are constructed by and for real estate developers" (p.33) providing evidence from Barcelona (1992), Atlanta (1996), Sydney (2000), Athens (2004) and Beijing (2000). Using the example of the 2010 Olympic Games, Shaw (2008) highlights how Vancouver followed a well-worn template for Olympic bidding, which started with developers securing the support of local politicians to start the 'leveraging' process which, he then argues, escalates to city and national level political support, as there is a recognition that resource commitments are significant if bids are to stand a chance of success.

Vancouver 2010: bid committee – harnessing elites

Of particular interest in terms of governance, public accountability and public investment is the way that the formal bid organisation is formed and formally constituted. In the example of Vancouver, the Vancouver-Whistler 2010 Olympic Bid Society was the first incarnation of the bid committee. This Bid Society, as Shaw (2008) highlights, was "a shortlisted who's who of developers, business interests and politicians" (p.6) which operated for a short period of time to garner support from business and some public monies to implant the idea that Vancouver could host the Winter Olympic Games. The Bid Society was replaced in 1999 by the Vancouver Whistler 2010 Bid Corporation (Bid Corp; it is telling that the word 'corporation' is front and centre here), which was the public facing, formally constituted body that ultimately fronted the bid for the 2010 Winter Olympics. Shaw (2008) highlights how the Bid Corp was chaired by Jack Poole, a well-known real estate developer in North America who, along with a Board of Directors, sought to secure the necessary political and financial support for the bid. The Bid Corp used the support of its business partners to secure the public support so crucial as part of bids now that the awarding body (the IOC) requires it. By 2002, the Bid Corp had local, provincial and federal government support, $34 million in cash and more in-kind support from public and private sources to run a campaign to win the 2010 Games. Both Shaw (2008) and Lenskyj (2010) have suggested that the promises made by the Bid Corp about what the Games would bring were open to critique. Specifically, claims that infrastructure projects central to likely bid success did not need to be costed into the bid were viewed as "misleading" (Shaw, 2008:14). Also, the significant security costs accompanying Olympic Games were also said to be under-estimated. Shaw (2008) finally highlights how the ill-informed are swept away on Bid Corp rhetoric, overlooking the fact that a number of Crown Corporations in British Columbia had "used their publicly derived money to back the bid" (p.25).

Bidding, transparency and accountability

Most concerning of all from the point of view of governance, ethics and impropriety is the fact that the host city bid committees (or corporations) for major sporting events (and to a degree other major events) are often separated or protected from meaningful democratic accountability for the decisions they make. For example, Shaw (2008) highlights how, until recently (as a result of *Olympic Agenda 2020*) the bid teams for Olympic Games had to pay $500,000 to the IOC once shortlisted and also had to demonstrate that they had enough resources left to produce a bid book and an associated advertising campaign to convince local, national and international audiences that their bid was the strongest. Again, there are governance, transparency and accountability issues when indirect public subsidy is being used to 'back the bid' – often a consumerist process designed to target quantity of 'support' without actual commitment to pay should the event be won (Foley, McGillivray & McPherson, 2012). As Shaw (2008) puts it, "the Bid Corp has $34 million in the bank, most of it public money to be used as necessary to convince the same public that it was a good idea to host the Games" (p.39). Moreover, Shaw highlights how the 'non-binding' plebiscite that was held in Vancouver as a measure of public opinion for the bid was also skewed in favour of the Olympic boosters, including use of public funds to promote the back the bid campaign, pro-bid media editorials on the day of the vote and bid supporting companies bussing their employees to the polling stations.

   Though much of the debate around event bidding processes focuses on financial impropriety and political machinations, there is also an important media element that should not be overlooked. Lenskyj (2008) has been outspoken in her critique of the relationship between the media industries and the Olympics. She suggests that, since the 1984 Olympic Games, this event has become attractive for journalists to cover and benefit from what others have called the 'Olympic Gravy Train'. Lenskyj (2008) provides examples from the Berlin 2000 Olympic bid and the successful Sydney 2000 Olympic bid to highlight how the media is increasingly bound into the bid machinery from the outset, ensuring that sympathetic stories are produced about the bid. She also provides evidence of mainstream media organisations supporting bid committees by providing links to their websites during the bid process, support not afforded to those alternative, independent media organisations seeking to alter the Olympic frame (Shaw, 2008) and communicate with a wider public. Finally, she argues that journalists often find themselves with significant conflicts of interest when being expected to report on the Olympic Games themselves whilst also being invited to Olympic booster, promotional events, as a result of their employers' status as a 'supporter' or 'partner' of the local Games bid.

Newman (2007) has also shown how the idea for the London 2012 Olympic bid was borne from the changing relationships of governance taking place in that city after 2000. The power of the elected Mayor was enhanced by the shared leadership roles that he enjoyed alongside the Prime Minister to satisfy the IOC's requirements; "the mayor in his own right is a signatory of the Olympic contract and this act implies readjustment of relationships. The Games give the mayor a world stage to promote the city and his own personal role in governing the city" (p.259). However, the potential for impropriety and corruption is increased when market-oriented influences on government are translated into private sector interests that influence the final Games bid. As Newman (2007) continues:

> the process of bidding for the Games continues well-worn roles for "big business" in the government of London... Businesses with London wide interests – the utility companies EDF Energy and BT, the airlines British Airways and Virgin Atlantic, and the management consultants Accenture – became "Premier Partners" of the Olympic Bid Committee.
>
> (p.260)

A picture emerges of corporate interests being at the heart of event bidding, as an illustration of urban entrepreneurial governance more generally. Politics and commerce become happy bedfellows as host cities seek to secure the sought after gold that boosters argue will derive from successful event bidding campaigns. Yet, there exists a lack of democratic accountability, especially at the early stages of bidding processes. Sponsors and other commercial partners appear able to hold democratic institutions to ransom in order to secure the investment required to launch and sustain a major event bid. In order to secure that support, state actors promise the opening up of opportunities for land purchase, lucrative construction projects and other business benefits. This, for Broudehoux & Sánchez (2015) reflects the "state-assisted privatization and commodification of the urban realm" (p.109) that mega events help facilitate. Whilst commercial involvement does not in itself mean that there will be impropriety or corruption (which may be defined in legal terms), there is evidence that constituting bid committees as corporate bodies does lead them to operate in a manner commensurate with private business despite being in receipt of significant public funds.

Conclusion

Global sport organisations were created as private gentlemen's clubs in the nineteenth century. There remains a legacy in their governance arrangements and legal status that has protected them from scrutiny in a manner that business and state organisations now experience as commonplace. In many respects, the two major sport event GSOs, FIFA and the IOC, have been able to operate without sanction in the way they have developed separate bidding processes for the award of the two most financially lucrative sporting events available. However, that freedom from national and international legal, ethical and commercial law has provided the environment within which impropriety and corruption has been able to thrive, both within these organisations (see recent FIFA and IOC scandals) and within those host city (or national) bidding organisations so desperate to secure the sought after prize of winning the rights to host either the FIFA World Cup or the Olympic Games. Throughout the 1980s and 1990s in particular, the IOC was mired in controversy, as its ability to pursue TPR meant it could establish distinct rules and standards of behaviour at odds with conventional policies and practices in other spheres of life. More recently, it has become clear that FIFA has also been operating in a similar manner, ultimately leading to the involvement of legal authorities and calls for major reforms of the bidding process for the FIFA World Cup. Though both GSOs have made public pronouncement about addressing their governance arrangements in respect of the bidding process for their event assets, as the commercial values of these events for a range of actors continue to grow, the temptation for politics and economics to come together in an unhealthy alliance continues to exist. Greater media attention and public outrage about the excesses of bidding contests and the systemic corruption existing within these GSOs may also exert pressure for greater accountability and transparency than has been possible through legal or political routes to date. What is clear is that, historically, the rules of the game have been known, but their interpretation by prospective hosts and members of the GSOs has been less than consistent.

References

Blakeley, G. (2010) Governing ourselves: Citizen participation and governance in Barcelona and Manchester. *International Journal of Urban and Regional Research*, 34(1), pp.130–145.

Brannagan, P. and Giulianotti, R. (2015) Soft power and soft disempowerment: Qatar, global sport and football's 2022 World Cup finals. *Leisure Studies*, 34(6), pp.703–719.

Broudehoux, A-M. and Sánchez, F. (2015) The politics of mega event planning in Rio de Janeiro: Contesting the Olympic City of Exception. In V. Viehoff and G. Poynter (eds), *Mega event cities: Urban legacies of global sport events* (pp.109–122). London: Routledge.

Calvert, J. and Blake, H. (2014) Plot to buy the World Cup. *The Sunday Times*, 1.

Eick, V. (2010) A neoliberal sports event? FIFA from the Estadio Nacional to the fan mile. *City*, 14(3), pp.278–297.

Foley, M., McGillivray, D. and McPherson, G. (2012) *Event policy: From theory to strategy*. London: Routledge.

Forster, J. (2016) Global sports governance and corruption. *Palgrave Communications*, 2, Article number: 15048.

Jennings, A. (2007) *Foul!: The secret world of FIFA*. London: HarperCollins.

Lauermann, J. (2016) Boston's Olympic bid and the evolving urban politics of event-led development. *Urban Geographies*, 37(2), pp.313–321.

Lenskyj, H. (2000) *Inside the Olympic Industry: Power, politics and activism*. Albany: SUNY.

Lenskyj, H. (2008) *Olympic industry resistance: Challenging Olympic power and propaganda*. Albany: SUNY.

Lenskyj, H. (2010) Olympic impacts on bid and host cities. In V. Girginov (ed.), *The Olympics: A critical reader*. London: Routledge.

Meier, H.E. and García, B. (2015) Protecting private transnational authority against public intervention: FIFA's power of national governments. *Public Administration*, 93(4), pp. 890–906.

Newman, P. (2007) 'Back the bid': The 2012 Summer Olympics and the governance of London. *Journal of Urban Affairs*, 29(3), pp.255–267.

Paton, K., Mooney, G. and McKee, K. (2012) Class, citizenship and regeneration: Glasgow and the Commonwealth Games 2014. *Antipode*, 44(4), pp.1470–1489.

Preuss, H. and Schnitzer, M. (2015) Organization costs for a Fifa World Cup and their significance during a bid. *Event Management*, 19(1), pp.57–72.

Rojek, C. (2013) *Event power: How global events manage and manipulate*. London: Sage.

Shaw, C.A. (2008) *Five rings circus: Myths and realities of the Olympic Games*. British Colombia, Canada: New Society Publishers.

Tomlinson, A. (2000) FIFA and the men who made it. *Soccer and Society*, 1(1), pp.55–71.

Waitt, G. (2001) The Olympic Spirit and civic boosterism: The Sydney 2000 Olympics. *Tourism Geographies*, 3(3), pp.249–278.

8
RESISTANCE AND ALTERNATIVE CAMPAIGNS

Introduction

Previously, we have shown how the increasing size and scale of cultural and sporting mega events have created an environment in which corruption and impropriety have been able to thrive. We highlighted how such corruption has led to increasing public awareness of the governance and ethical challenges posed by major events. Moving on from this, we now consider the increasing prevalence of protest and resistance movements accompanying bids for peripatetic events. This chapter assesses the key motivations for those looking to oppose or protest against event bids, the strategies employed by successful movements and how bid campaigns have engaged, successfully and unsuccessfully, with groups in an attempt to mitigate their impact. Focus will be given to the growing interconnectedness of oppositional groups and associations, the acceleration of protest campaigns mediated through social networks, the increasing digital mediation of protest and resistance and the narratives employed by such groups to challenge bid orthodoxies.

Event bids, democratic deficits and legitimation crises

> MEs [mega events] are meant to generate a de-politicized atmosphere of consensus, enjoyment and entertainment, from which any political disturbance must be eliminated. Consistent with the ancient tradition of the Olympic truce, the ME must be a pure pacifier, essentially beyond politics, conflict and protest...yet, at the same time MEs are increasingly becoming the stage of ever-greater expressions of public protest.
> *(Pavoni, 2015:475)*

Foley, McGillivray & McPherson (2012) have argued that as events are incorporated into boosterist strategies, designed to assuage the multiple and complex problems associated with de-industrialisation in advanced western liberal democracies in particular, there are consequences in terms of the amplification of democratic deficits or legitimation crises. In particular, sporting mega events have become implicated in a neoliberalising agenda (Brenner & Theodore, 2005) that prevails across the world:

> private capital now has significant influence over the development, planning and regulatory functions associated with major sporting events…as the local state is increasingly required (of economic necessity within the logic of neo-liberal urbanism) to dance to the tune of major sponsors in bidding for and delivering events, there is a knock-on effect for 'local' stakeholder interests (whether citizens or businesses).
>
> *(Foley et al., 2012:73)*

Waitt (2001) has argued that sporting mega event bids, talking principally about the Sydney 2000 Olympics, represent propaganda exercises, designed to imbue social consensus through the vehicle of spectacle. Certainly, the promotional campaigns employed by bidding teams when seeking public support increasingly resemble major product launches or experiential marketing initiatives more common in the corporate world (see Chapter 6). As argued in Chapter 3, the formation of public–private growth coalitions, business-led bid teams largely unaccountable to local taxpayers, further reinforces the shift to an entrepreneurial over welfare agenda in local politics. Lenskyj (2002) has argued that in relation to sporting mega event bids the 'terms of the debate' are framed by Olympic boosters and their public relations consultants leaving community groups and other resident interests largely invisible and powerless, at least in terms of media exposure and in public response.

Andranovich, Burbank & Heying (2001) have also been critical of the so-called urban entrepreneurial turn. They argue that local business-led networks and coalitions conceive of bids, provide them with the required seed funding, and then ensure their interests are embedded in the urban development processes that are initiated as a result. Müller (2015) reinforces this point, arguing that what he calls the mega event *syndrome* leads to a number of symptoms and consequences for cities. Two of these symptoms are the event 'takeover', and the event 'fix', wherein the requirements of event bidding processes (laid out by awarding bodies) lead to event priorities becoming planning priorities (takeover), and the needs of the event displacing urban infrastructure needs more generally. Second, proponents of event bids overestimate the potential for the mega event to produce 'fixes' for major planning challenges, and resources are similarly redirected to support initiatives that benefit the event (bid and delivery). Focusing on the ideas of circulation and flows through the urban realm, Gaffney (2015) also suggests that, in the very act of bidding, aspiring hosts court the event owner (or awarding body), highlighting how their bid will enable free circulation through the city (e.g. high quality hotels, specific Games lanes), often facilitated by amendments to existing planning and trading standards legislation (see also Smith, 2014, 2015).

Another feature of the mega event syndrome that Müller (2015) identifies is the temptation to overestimate benefits and the need to invest public resources to support, in the main, private interests at the bid stage and beyond. Framed in this way, event bids are, inevitably, focused around impressing a cadre of external actors, whether the awarding body (e.g. FIFA, the IOC, the Commonwealth Games Federation) or the target markets of international visitors, investors and workers that the host destination hopes to attract in the future. In other words, the right brand message, communicated through an ambitious bid vision, becomes more important than securing the consent of the host resident population. In a period marked by intense inter-urban competition, effective destination brand strategies take precedence over addressing systemic inequalities of wealth and income within the host destination itself. The argument goes that by communicating (through bids) a geography of hope (that your city will be dynamic, vibrant, affluent, cosmopolitan), the positive impressions accrued will lead to endless benefits (socially, culturally and economically) for the host population.

As a consequence, over-estimating the benefits and viewing the event opportunity as a 'fix' or 'takeover' leads to the adoption of a particular set of approaches to engagement with internal audiences in the host destination. Although mega event sanctioning bodies now require 'public opinion' assessments to be made by bid organisations, resident input into bid processes has historically been minimal, beyond the easy consumption choice of backing the bid via the click of a button (Foley et al., 2012). As Waitt (1999) argues, with reference to the Sydney 2000 bid process, "the only form of public participation in the bidding process were opinion polls. Evident in the Sydney bid is the triumph of the entrepreneurial over public participation and the image over substance" (p.1057). Of principal concern to those people who oppose event bids is the false premise on which 'support' is secured. Prospective event hosts submit a bid book detailing the outcomes the sanctioning body can expect should they be successful in their application to host. Many commentators have likened the bid book for mega sporting events to a work of fiction (Müller, 2015) or a glossy prospectus for what a host might wish to do to transform its urban fabric and economic ambitions. And yet, back the bid campaigns invariably set out to secure public support without providing full information to those who will bear the brunt of the 'costs' associated with delivering on the promises made in the bid book, and these are indeed promises, as the bid book commitment forms the basis of the host city contract that accompanies the awarding of a major sporting (and cultural) event. As local bid committees are often separated from direct accountability to the taxpayers of the city or nation (see Chapter 7), there exists a *legitimation deficit* whereby the public that pays has little power (other than through public opinion surveys) to contest the basis on which the bid is made. Moreover, there is little incentive for those promoting prospective events to lay out the true costs likely to accrue from bidding and winning an event. As Müller (2015) has suggested, outlining the true costs of hosting a sporting mega event could compromise the ability to garner public support locally and nationally. For these reasons, there is a tendency for public bodies to manage carefully the extent of information released about who will actually have to bear the burden of deficits should an event ultimately be a failure and not return the riches proposed by the awarding bodies and their partners. And yet, historically, event bids have generated protest, dissent and opposition, though their levels of success vary markedly.

Opposing events: a historical perspective

Events have long been understood as both a means to extend social control, containing unruly populations, as well as providing a space where dominant culture is challenged (Rojek, 2005; Schechner, 1995). For example, Carnival has, historically, offered people a temporary escape route where inverted hierarchies were celebrated (Gilmore, 1998), and yet, like the major sporting spectacles of today, these events remained tied to a conventional social order where "official culture smiles as it asks ordinary people to confirm the existing power structures" (Schechner, 1995:83). Events can be considered temporary disruptions to existing arrangements and the same can be said of the role of public protests around proposed major event bids, protests that are managed and scheduled to suit the needs of an elite group of event promoters.

Pavoni (2015) suggests that the freedom to engage in urban protest is being eroded everywhere, and yet the conditions driving it, including social, economic and political inequalities mean that expressions of discontent are "erupting everywhere" (p.475). These conditions, though perhaps intensified in a period of hypercapitalism are not new and here we highlight how major sporting events, in particular, have been a site of contestation for decades, but that the nature of the opposition and its expression has changed markedly. Lenskyj (2008) argues that local activists, community leaders, elected representatives (often of opposition parties) and journalists are normally at the heart of scrutinising bid processes within host cities. Anti-Olympic Committees have been around for some time, from the relatively unstructured and disorganised protests found at the Mexico 1968 Olympic Games onwards. Over time, organised protest has been formalised into committee structures (see Torino 2006 Anti-Olympics), though 'success' has been inconsistent, at best. These groups have tended to focus attention on the principal beneficiaries of sporting mega events – real estate interests, construction firms, advertising and marketing agencies, sponsors and the political elites (Whitson & Horne, 2006; Shaw 2012; Müller, 2015) and on how Olympic Games bids have been used by developers to secure public subsidy to target land in potentially profitable urban locations. They also, as in the case of the Salt Lake City 2002 Winter Olympic Games included minority, anti-poverty, women's and disability rights groups concerned about housing and civil liberties protections. And yet, the 'impact' of the tapestry of interest groups on preventing, or even amending event bid strategies has been limited.

The difficulties facing watchdogs, community groups and activists in having their views heard can be traced back to the anti-globalisation protests of the late 1990s, particularly in Seattle. Following these protests, there was, as Lenskyj (2002) has described, a clampdown on public protests that also impacted on the visibility of anti-Olympic activity prior to the Sydney 2000 Olympics and at subsequent Olympic Games. An increasing securitisation of urban civic space is a feature of mega event hosting (Jennings, 2010), but this also affects the rights of activist groups and local residents to publicly oppose bid committee proposals well before a bid is actually considered. The stakes are high for event promoters who have often gambled with their political futures to bring the Games to their destination and they are hostile to the possibility that 'minority' interests may impede access to the rewards accruable from urban transformation.

However, despite the conditions for public protest being constrained, since 2008 there has been a noticeable increase in both the number of oppositional campaigns in operation and, crucially, their *modus operandi*. Additionally, there is both a global and a local element to these intimations of opposition that require further consideration. At the macro/global level, it is safe to say that the legitimacy of sporting mega events (the Olympics and the FIFA World Cup, in particular) in achieving positive political, economic, social, cultural and environmental impacts has been subject to intense critique, since the 2008 Summer Games were awarded to Beijing (Boykoff, 2014; Coaffee, 2014; Raco, 2014; Zimbalist, 2015). Central to this trend is a growing body of evidence, in academic, policy and activist/independent media circles, of the adverse effects generated by sporting mega events for a variety of publics. Well-documented cost overruns (Zimbalist, 2015), accusations of corruption in the sporting event governance system (Meier & García, 2015; Forster, 2016), unfulfilled promises on material legacies (economic return, jobs, transport infrastructure), and evidence of deleterious social impacts (Finkel, 2015), including human rights abuses (Adams & Piekarz, 2015) and exploitation (Finkel & Matheson, 2015), have drawn more attention than ever to the potential failures of sporting mega events as a panacea for urban regeneration.

Protesting the bid

At the local level, global messages about extravagance, gigantism, corporate gain (over citizen benefit) and corruption have led to the establishment of oppositional groups that have as their *raison d'être* the suspension of a bid candidacy. Recent examples include the No Halifax group that contributed to the Canadian city's withdrawal from the bidding process to host the 2014 Commonwealth Games (which was eventually hosted in Glasgow, Scotland). The well-established Toronto 'Bread Not Circuses' Coalition successfully opposed Toronto's plans to enter the Olympic bidding campaign in both 1996 and 2008 – building on more general antipathy in Canada towards mega events since the (in)famous Montreal 1976 cost overruns. Of even greater importance is the entry of sophisticated coalitions of interest groups, brought together under an umbrella entity to campaign for the suspension of bidding proposals or demanding that these proposals are at least subject to a test of public opinion via a local or national referendum.

In recent years there has also been a change in the way opposition, dissent or protest towards event bids has been organised and mobilised, which is having some potentially significant impacts on the bidding process itself (what awarding bodies require) and on the practices of prospective host bidding teams thereafter. No longer is it possible for a potential host (in the advanced liberal democracies, at least) to attract powerful influencers externally with promises of extravagant spectacles without having to account for this investment to an (increasingly) sceptical public. In fact, domestic consent for the right to bid for a sporting mega event on behalf of the electorate is becoming more and more difficult to secure. In the bid process for the 2022 Winter Olympic Games, the IOC had to cope with the withdrawal of three candidate cities on the basis of either public referendum or significant popular opposition. The 2024 Olympic Games bidding process has also seen a number of high profile casualties on the basis of a lack of public support (Boston, Hamburg and Budapest all withdrawing).

We can, perhaps now talk of more organised protest movements, embedded locally, but with a transnational coordination (and impact) that enables them to contest the approach to urban development policy that mega events reflect, rather than the ethos of the mega event *per se* (i.e. not against the universal values associated with them). So, for example, as Boston's political and business leaders sought to secure the US Olympic Committee nomination to become the national candidate city for the 2024 Olympic Games, the two principal issues of concern were: (i) the lack of transparency in the decision to bid in the first place, and (ii) the burden of development costs falling on the taxpayers of that city. Concerns over the value (and values) of major sporting event development projects and their expression through protest and resistance are inseparable from the broader anti-corporate movement, given further sustenance by the global financial crisis of 2008. Those considering bidding for major sporting (and other) events cannot now avoid the shadow of largesse associated with unaccountable global corporations, and the principal sporting mega event awarding bodies are tarnished with similar accusations.

Hiller & Wanner (2011) have also demonstrated that public opinion has become a more important constituent element in the decision to award sporting mega events (beyond simply the technical proficiency detailed in the bid book). For example, from the Torino Winter Olympics onwards, measures of public opinion (polls or referenda) have been desired and, latterly, required as part of the bidding process as a result of the IOC's *Olymbic Agenda 2020*. Though Hiller & Wanner (2015) argue that there is little evidence that low(er) public opinion was a decisive factor in successful or unsuccessful bids, the initiation of public polling has become an important tool for those seeking to oppose the very act of bidding on behalf of the host city. Shaw (2008) substantiates this view, suggesting that it is now more possible than ever before to 'break the Olympic frame', stressing that "active resistance begins with awareness" (p.263). Drawing on the example of Vancouver 2010 (and his role within the NO GAMES 2010 movement), he demonstrates how local bid organisers (he calls them 'promoters') seek to protect the dominant Olympic frame, of "elite sport for peaceful cooperation amongst the nations; goodies for the host city" (p.264). However, he also describes how oppositional groups can break the frame by utilising the mainstream media to draw attention to what the Olympics is actually about:

The IOC is in the business of marketing sport for television by showing cute young athletes in Spandex/Gortex; the local bid corp is composed of real estate developers who likely don't give a tinker's damn about sports but see in the Olympics a way to advance their pet projects with public money under the smoke and mirrors of the IOCs big circus tent.

(p.265)

Shaw argues that oppositional groups need to be radical in their rejection of the dominant Olympic frame, otherwise they will lose mainstream media interest at the beginning and will secure no concessions from the IOC, thereafter. He also suggests that it is becoming much easier for those sceptical of the value of the Olympics, for a host of political, social and economic reasons, to coalesce online, sharing information and tactics with each other in a host destination, but perhaps more importantly sharing across territories.

Protest and resistance: mediated opposition

Social 'movements' around major sport events have developed and they now frequently form coalitions with those interest groups sharing a 'broadly' common set of values and goals. To be successful, it is necessary for these groups to develop a physical manifestation of opposition alongside a digitally mediated opposition and to do so with organisation, leadership and excellent communication strategies.

McGillivray & Jones (2013) have suggested that alongside a renewed interest in protest, dissent and opposition to major sport events from special interest groups, charitable organisations and those concerned with the additional tax burdens falling on the host city populace, have come new methods for the coordination and organisation of protest – which they argue have also become 'events' in themselves. Pavoni (2015) has also suggested that the mega spectacle of events, requires *event-generation* – arousing interest from the public in having an event, and *event-neutralisation* – ensuring that the 'dangers' of collective public interest do not lead to negative spillover effects. These ideas are relevant to how event bids are managed to avoid the expression of opposition and protest. New(er) forms of media are now frequently used by event promoters to arouse the interest of the public to 'back the bid', whilst intense monitoring of negative stories is also carried out, often using the power of official media partners to deny discursive space to alternative voices.

Some of these methods are consistent with previous practices around the colonisation of public spaces (e.g. sit ins and demonstrations), but new techniques made available by the affordances of digital technologies and platforms have provided the possibility of reaching new audiences, organising across a broader network public (Boyd, 2014) and hijacking or seizing the event platform (Price, 2008) in such a way that the small and relatively powerless (in terms of access to media space) can turn the tables on the powerful. Loosely formed collectives, created for the purpose of opposing major event bids (and therefore temporary and ephemeral for that reason), operate and, in many cases, sometimes continue to exist beyond the narrow issue agenda they were originally formed for – what we term the *professionalisation of opposition*. We are not suggesting that digital opposition represents a panacea of protest (McGillivray & Jones, 2013), but existing power brokers are having to re-think the techniques they use to secure consent when faced with a new threat that is more difficult to suppress than simply enacting legislative powers to outlaw public protest in designated public spaces, as happened in Beijing in the lead up to and during the 2008 Olympic Games.

Moreover, the ubiquitous diffusion of networked social media has been extremely important in opening up space to contest dominant power elites. Social media facilitate a reach and access to large audiences that provide at least the potential for dominant boosterist narratives to be contested. Having agreements with mainstream media partners does not protect bid committees from critique, as a cacophony of voices can be released that are more difficult to manage and control, a feature of digital deterritorialisation in action. Though anxious to avoid overemphasising their power, social media have the potential to facilitate "the organization, mobilization and globalization of social protest" (Pavoni, 2015, p.479). This is mainly because social media platforms and their affordances enable more nimble and viral possibilities for protest with an immediacy and counter-cultural style which is alien to the corporate bidding machine. That said, to counter this threat to narrative control, bid committees are calling on digital marketing expertise to neutralise the disruptive potential of digital and social media.

Lenskyj (2010) draws attention to the culpability of the mainstream media in signing up to support bids and, therefore, removing an important vehicle for oppositional groups to have their views heard. As she argues, when referring to the 2002 Salt Lake City bribery scandal, the local newspapers found themselves facing a conflict of interests:

> they occupied two roles, as objective reporters of the Olympic Games and as participants in "Olympic Spirit" promotional events. Similar conflicts existed when major television networks, newspapers and sport magazines paid millions of dollars for the honour of calling themselves Olympic suppliers, donors, sponsors and/or rights holders.
>
> *(p.376)*

Mainstream or established media, have been less than helpful at drawing attention to the views of activists, community groups and even those of critical elected representatives (Shaw, 2008). In contrast, independent media organisations have been active in providing oppositional voices with a media platform to have their concerns aired. These independent media included Salt Lake City's *Democracy Now* grassroots public radio station (Lenskyj, 2010), and the Athens 2004 athens.indymedia.org and anti2004.net sites. Scrutinising the London 2012 bid process was No London 2012 and its follow up Games Monitor (www.gamesmonitor.org), which has continually acted as a research body, discussion forum, process and political body to combat what is viewed as the complicity of other agencies in supporting the Olympic bid. Each of these media platforms or spaces is different, but they share features in the way they have used emerging digital and social media platforms to project their dissent, protest and resistance. There is also some anecdotal evidence emerging that the mainstream is running with critical articles on mega event bids (Boston 2024 is a good example). The impetus for these articles often comes from smaller oppositional groups who operate as fact checkers before presenting stories to the more established media outlet with an existing 'reach'.

For critical commentators, an explosion of content online relating (loosely) to protest or oppositional voices (e.g. via Twitter, Facebook and blogs), does not necessarily result in material progress for the specific cause. There is a significant amount of information circulating around major sports events in particular that could be considered to be occupying an oppositional position, including Games Monitor, Counter Olympics Network (@counterOlympics) and Rio On Watch (RioOnWatch.org). These organisations seek to hold organisers, bid committees, local and central governments to account as they challenge organisers' use of social media as a promotional tool with their own powerful counter stories that often rely on other social media web platforms such as YouTube, Instagram and Twitter to evidence a very different reality for the proposed beneficiaries. The political–corporate–media complex is now invariably challenged to defend its position against what we might call a new media activism that generates its own content and audiences without having to go through existing media channels.

No Boston Olympics

The new oppositional movements contesting event bids are well-organised, loose coalitions of (sometimes quite diverse) individuals and groups, coalescing around internet-mediated campaigns. They use the very polls designed to garner public support on behalf of the organisers to contest it. The efforts of the No Boston Olympic group (and to a lesser extent their No Boston 2024 counterparts) provide a successful recent example. Crucial to the success of those opposing the Boston 2014 Olympic bid (in that the bid did not ultimately go forward) was their ability to meld together a relatively disparate range of interests into collective offline activities, whilst generating online mobilisation using web, alternative media and social media platforms, which ultimately led to extensive mainstream media coverage. As Shaw (2008) has suggested, the "center of gravity for the opposition is their ability to get their message out there into the world. If it makes news future access to the media will grow rather than shrink" (p.265). Making the news in this way also takes the opposition out of the margins and into the centre of political debate, which can lead to the event awarding body (or, in Boston's case, the US National Olympic Committee) pulling back from becoming embroiled in a potentially damaging campaign. The No Boston Olympics group became well known in the lead up to the suspension of the city's candidacy, organising a very active social media campaign, but also appearing regularly on network television to debate with bid supporters, taking the No Boston 2024 message out to a wider audience. The group's charismatic leadership and 'young professional' status (Malone, 2015) also helped negate the fear that oppositional groups were in some way radical, left-of-centre naysayers. This group was effective in the way in which it penetrated the consciousness of the public, to the extent that it was more recognisable than the bid organisation itself by the end of the campaign (Lauermann, 2016). Finally, its effectiveness was grounded on more traditional opposition tactics of "(1) calling for transparency in the bid corporation and (2) highlighting the public subsidies which the bid organization has downplayed" (Lauermann, 2016:6). However, it was the amplification of the negative messages using sophisticated social media techniques that ultimately generated the traction with the wider public that led to Mayor Walsh withdrawing Boston's candidacy.

The No Boston Olympics case is also interesting because it provides evidence that oppositional groups are now able to demonstrate a degree of global solidarity to their activities and actions, which suggests that this movement represents a real threat to the future sustainability of awarding bodies' activities. For example, the No Boston 2024 group travelled to Germany to support their European comrades in opposing the Hamburg 2024 bid, leading to a majority 'no' vote in that city's referendum. In responding to the failure of the Hamburg bid, No Boston 2024 commented "Citizens across the globe are saying loudly and clearly that they have more important priorities than throwing a three-week party for the undemocratic, unaccountable International Olympic Committee (IOC)" (Butler, 2015 [online]).

Not only does this represent a new challenge to the sanctioning bodies in each candidate city, but more importantly, it reflects a change whereby *oppositional consultants* are now operating in direct counterpoint to the various experts employed by bidding host cities. This explains why, when asked whether post-award oppositional groups can still win, NO GAMES 2010 responded, "locally, no; globally, yes" (Shaw, 2008: 266). In other words, the opposition may not win the initial fight, but they can perfect tactics that others can learn from to ensure that they can more effectively prevent a successful bid, rather than face a rearguard action once the Games are awarded. Accountability for taxpayers is being sought earlier, and oppositional movements are forming sooner, than ever before. There are intimations of a global solidarity emerging where protest movements from one bid cycle inform and work alongside their contemporaries in other cities or nations. In essence, the act of protest is being professionalised with strategies and tactics being shared in a similar way to how bid committees operate.

Recognising limits: opposition, protest and the status quo

Our reading of power is that it is multidimensional, not simply a possession deployed by the powerful against the powerless, but rather a force that conditions what is possible, permitting certain actions, behaviours and subject positions to operate whilst disqualifying others. In the context of major events, Müller (2015) has highlighted the power of the neo-liberalised order to narrowly frame the conditions of possibility for how mega events can be conceived in the urban environment. Similarly, Gaffney (2015) has stressed how sporting mega events are enablers of more intensive capital accumulation, enabling certain flows and circulations through the city and disabling others. Finally, Pavoni (2015) suggests that 'transgressions' (in the sense of opposition or protest) are tolerated within mega event narratives, as long as they remain micro, temporary and fail to "provoke challenges to the status quo" (p.476). So, whilst on one level, the examples provided in this chapter highlight the capability of oppositional campaigns to lead to successful outcomes in terms of withdrawal of bids (e.g. Boston and Hamburg), or in hijacking the platform to secure media coverage that awakens a sleeping public, we need to be careful not to overestimate the longer-term impacts of these momentary or fleeting transgressions on the contours of major events going forward. Shaw (2008) in his powerful critique of the Olympic Games, and the Vancouver 2010 Olympic Games in particular, recognises that the Games went ahead despite popular protests taking place in the city. Major event narratives are defined by struggle, contestation and negotiation and whilst our focus here on bidding means that it is pre-delivery that most interests us, it is clear that even once a peripatetic event is won, there is space for ongoing disruption to the status quo and to the dominant narrative.

Pavoni (2015) actually suggests that *resistant legacies* could be one of the most powerful outcomes of sporting mega events. Though he refers to the conflict and opposition that is a feature of the event once won, the idea can just as easily be applied to the pre-event bidding process. There is some evidence that this is already happening with the recent examples of Olympic bids being withdrawn due to the efforts of coordinated local, national and, on occasion, transnational groups and organisations:

> [C]onflict is not only a potential disruption to the ME's legacy and impact, but may be generative of legacies of its own: not merely disruptive, it is also productive of alternative forms of urban life that directly challenge the logic underlining capitalist urbanization…regardless of its visible outcome, the protest, as a manifestation of urban conflict, has in itself the potential to reshape the social, affective and normative fabric of the city.
>
> *(p.482)*

So, when thinking about where protest and opposition have a place within the event bidding process, we can see that there is more space now available for competing claims and narratives to 'unsettle, subvert and make uncomfortable' the deployment of power, especially when the mechanisms for deploying power are less easily fixed, as online spaces can be effectively used to destabilise existing architectures, infrastructures and institutional environments (McGillivray & Jones, 2013). Crucially, there is some evidence that the opposition is organising earlier and with more strategic intentions than was previously the case (Lauermann, 2016).

Conclusions

Event bids generate opposition from a variety of actors. Historically, expressions of opposition to bidding for an Olympic Games, a FIFA World Cup or even a peripatetic cultural event have varied in their organisation, mobilisation, visibility and, ultimately, success. At worst, oppositional groups have failed to advance their arguments and have been relegated to the margins of the debate. They have failed to impact the event frame and, faced with powerful promotional interests, have been unable to sustain coordinated opposition or to effect change. However, in this chapter we have argued that there is evidence that opposition to major event bids is becoming more effective, globally coordinated and increasingly (social) media savvy. Drawing on public discontent over the costs of bids, lack of transparency in decision making and concerns over the liabilities that may fall upon citizens in the long term, organised movements are now forming not only *within* each host bidding destination but also *between* them. It would be naïve to assume that small victories will necessarily result in longer-term 'successes', but we can be confident that bid committees and their partners are now being held to account in a more systematic manner than perhaps was the case in previous decades.

References

Adams, A. and Piekarz, M. (2015) Sport events and human rights: Positive promotion or negative erosion? *Journal of Policy Research in Tourism, Leisure & Events*, 7(3), pp.220–236.

Andranovich, G., Burbank, M.J. and Heying, C.H. (2001) Olympic cities: Lessons learned from mega-event politics. *Journal of Urban Affairs*, 23(2), pp.113–131.

Boyd, D. (2014) *It's complicated: The social lives of networked teens*. London: Yale University Press.

Boykoff, J. (2014) *Celebration capitalism and the Olympic games*. London: Routledge.

Brenner, N. and Theodore, N. (2005) Neoliberalism and the urban condition. *City*, 9(1), pp.101–107.

Butler, N. (2015) Hamburg 2024 blow shows Thomas Bach remains out of touch with what ordinary citizens want. Available at http://www.insidethegames.biz/articles/1032139/nick-butler-hamburg-2024-blow-shows-thomas-bach-remains-out-of-touch-with-what-ordinary-citizens-want (accessed 31 March 2017).

Coaffee, J. (2014) The uneven geographies of the Olympic carceral: From exceptionalism to normalisation. *The Geographical Journal*. Advance online publication. doi:10.1111/geoj.12081.

Finkel, R. (2015) Introduction to Special Issue on Social Justice and Events-related Policy. *Journal of Policy Research in Tourism, Leisure & Events*, 7(3), pp.217–219.

Finkel, R. and Matheson, C. (2015) Landscape of commercial sex before the 2010 Vancouver Winter Games. *Journal of Policy Research in Tourism, Leisure & Events*, 7(3), pp.251–265

Foley, M., McGillivray, D. and McPherson, G. (2012) *Event policy: From theory to strategy*. London: Routledge.

Forster, J. (2016) Global sports governance and corruption. *Palgrave Communications*, 2, Article number 15048.

Gaffney, C. (2015) Gentrifications in pre-Olympic Rio de Janeiro. *Urban Geography*, 37(8), pp.1132–1153.

Gilmore, D.D. (1998) *Carnival and culture*. London: Yale University Press.

Hiller, H.H. and Wanner, R.A. (2011) Public opinion in host Olympic Cities: The case of the 2010 Vancouver Winter Games. *Sociology*, 45(5), pp.883–899.

Hiller, H.H. and Wanner, R.A. (2015) The psycho-social impact of the Olympics as urban festival: A leisure perspective. *Leisure Studies*, 34(6), pp.672–688.

Jennings, W. (2010) Governing the Games in an age of uncertainty: The Olympics and organisational responses to risk. In A. Richards, P. Fussey and A. Silke (eds), *Terrorism and the Olympics: Major event security and lessons for the future* (pp.135–162). London: Routledge.

Lauermann, J. (2016) Boston's Olympic bid and the evolving urban politics of event-led development. *Urban Geographies*, 37(2), pp.313–321.

Lenskyj, H. (2002) International Olympic resistance: Thinking globally, acting locally. *Proceedings of the Sixth International Symposium for Olympic Research*, pp.205–208.

Lenskyj, H. (2008) *Olympic Industry resistance: Challenging Olympic power and propaganda*. Albany: SUNY Press.

Lenskyj, H. (2010) Olympic impacts on bid and host cities. In V. Girginov (ed.), *The Olympics: A critical reader*. London: Routledge.

Malone, S. (2015) Boston activist group credited for defeating Olympics pitch. Available at http://www.reuters.com/article/usa-olympics-boston-idUSL1N1081AG20150728?irpc=932 (accessed 26 October 2016).

McGillivray, D. and Jones, J. (2013) Events and resistance. In R. Finkel, D. McGillivray, G. McPherson and P. Robinson (eds), *Research themes for events*, Oxon: CABI.

Meier, H.E. and García, B. (2015) Protecting private transnational authority against public intervention: FIFA's power of national governments. *Public Administration*, 93(4), pp.890–906.

Müller, M. (2015) The mega-event syndrome: Why So much goes wrong in mega-event planning and what to do about it. *Journal of the American Planning Association*, 81(1), pp.6–17.

Pavoni, A. (2015) Resistant legacies. *Annals of Leisure Research*, 18(4), pp.470–490.

Price, M. (2008) On seizing the Olympic platform. In M.E. Price and D. Dayan (eds), *Owning the Olympics: Narratives of the new China* (pp.86–114). Michigan: Digitalculturebooks.

Raco, M. (2014) Delivering flagship projects in an era of regulatory capitalism: State-led privatization and the London Olympics 2012. *International Journal of Urban & Regional Research*, 38(1), pp.176–197.

Rojek, C. (2005) *Leisure theory: Principles and practice*. Basingstoke: Palgrave Macmillan.

Schechner, R. (1995) *The future of ritual: Writings on culture and performance*. London: Routledge.

Shaw, C.A. (2008) *Five rings circus: Myths and realities of the Olympic Games*. British Colombia, Canada: New Society Publishers.

Shaw, C.A. (2012) The economics and marketing of the Olympic Games from bid phase to aftermath. In H.J. Lenskyj and S. Wagg (eds), *The Palgrave handbook of Olympic studies* (pp.248–260). New York: Palgrave.

Smith, A. (2014) Leveraging sport mega-events: New model or convenient justification? *Journal of Policy Research in Tourism, Leisure and Events*, 6(1), pp.15–30.

Smith, A. (2015) *Events in the City: Using Public Spaces as Event Venues*. London: Routledge.

Waitt, G. (1999) Playing games with Sydney: Marketing Sydney for the 2000 Olympics. *Urban Studies*, 36(7), pp.1055–1077.

Waitt, G. (2001) The Olympic Spirit and civic boosterism: The Sydney 2000 Olympics. *Tourism Geographies*, 3(3), pp.249–278.

Whitson, D. and Horne, J. (2006) Underestimated costs and overestimated benefits? Comparing the outcomes of sports mega-events in Canada and Japan. *Sociological Review*, 54(2), pp.71–89.

Zimbalist, A. (2015) *Circus Maximus: The economic gamble behind hosting the Olympics and the World Cup*. Washington, DC: Brookings Institution Press.

PART IV

Case studies in event bidding

9

RIO'S 2016 OLYMPIC BID

Putting South America on the map

Introduction

This chapter focuses on the city of Rio de Janeiro's bid for the 2016 Olympic Games. Drawing on the three main pillars of the book, attention is first paid to the *politics* underpinning the bid, including the rationale for bidding, and the political, economic and social circumstances in Rio (and Brazil) at that time. Second, the chapter illustrates the approaches to *persuasion* adopted by the Rio bid organisers, including the key narratives developed, the technical promises made and the campaigning tactics employed. Finally, the chapter draws attention to the (limited) expressions of *opposition and resistance* to the bid, and concludes by drawing out some insights from the Rio bid for future bid campaigns.

Rationale for bidding: social and economic transformation

There is much debate about the circumstances that led to the city of Rio bidding for the rights to host the 2016 Olympic Games. Scholars critical of the use of sporting mega events as a key feature of urban re-structuring point to Rio as an exemplary case study of these processes in action (Gaffney, 2015; Broudehoux & Sánchez, 2015). Well before Rio actually submitted its bid to the IOC in 2009, Broudehoux & Sánchez (2015) suggest that there were several macro economic and political drivers that influenced the decision to pursue an Olympic bid. Most crucial of these was the adoption of a 'strategic planning approach' in the city, based on a neo-liberal mode of governance that shifted the focus of public investment to "improving the city's image, repackaging its assets and marketing its competitive advantage in order to attract foreign investors, wealthy residents, international tourists and agents of the new creative class" (Broudehoux & Sánchez, 2015:110). Gaffney (2015) argues that coalitions of political, business and sporting actors had been committed to pursuing sporting mega events since the 1990s as a facet of public policy. Political leaders bought into the promise of greater external investment, tourist visitation and global recognition as features of a choice development strategy (Broudehoux & Sánchez, 2015), and sporting mega events aligned well with that desire to initiate and become the engine for the increasing involvement of non-state actors in the reconfiguration of the city. Outside Rio itself, Brazil was also viewed as one of the fastest growing BRIC nations in the late 1990s and early 2000s, which gave further sustenance to the Olympic bid – the opportunity for Rio (and Brazil) to showcase its success to the world and build upon its rapid economic development.

Whilst sporting mega events are not perceived as the panacea, the fact that bidding deadlines are tight intensifies these processes and enables key actors to secure planning commitments and land use amendments that become contractual obligations once the bid is submitted – and ultimately victorious. There was a recognition in Rio that bidding for the Games provided an opportunity to initiate improvements to the city's urban fabric, including transportation, its dilapidated port area and other locations in the city requiring significant infrastructural development in order to be able to attract and service the needs of tourists and investors. Gaffney (2015) argues that an overarching event strategy was used to justify a wide range of political, economic, and social changes that elites sought to introduce in Rio. There was also a 'rare' (in Rio's case) political alignment involving municipal, provincial and federal levels of government. The key political actors at each level formed alliances to strengthen Rio's case, with President Lula, state governor Sergio Cabral and Rio's Mayor, Eduardo Paes, working closely to advance Rio's case with the key influencers within the IOC.

Rio's bid for the Olympic Games in 2016 cannot be separated from its other forays into the sporting mega event field. Firstly, from as early as 1999 – linked to the adoption of the choice development strategy Rio decided to bid for the 2007 Pan American Games (a multi-sport event) rather than attempt to secure the 2008 Olympic Games. In 2002, Rio was awarded the 2007 Pan American Games and this provided the city with the foundation to build both its technical (new stadia development) and narrative case for future sporting mega event bids, including being a host city for the 2014 FIFA World Cup. Rio had also secured the rights to host the 2013 FIFA Confederations Cup in advance of the successful FIFA World Cup bid. Rio's bid for the Olympic Games was the culmination of a planned, long-term strategy of urban development. Its key political and business actors made the scholarship case for Rio, indicating that hosting the biggest sporting mega event possible would allow partial transformations to be turned into permanent and long lasting ones.

Bid narrative: South America's turn

On successfully being awarded the rights to host the Olympic Games in 2016, the bid committee President, Carloz Arthur Nuzman, reinforced three main pillars (or narratives). These were: technical competence in all areas; promotion of a unique experience for all participants; and transformation of both the city and the country. Rio successfully made the case that it possessed the capability to deliver the technical infrastructures required to host the Olympics because of its strategic investment in venues, transportation and accommodation for the 2007 Pan American Games and construction commitments that had been made as part of the successful bid to become a 2014 FIFA World Cup host city – where the famous Maracana Stadium was to be, essentially, rebuilt. Rio also seized every opportunity to remind the IOC that it was the best placed of all bidding cities to provide the financial return expected because of its position as an emerging economic superpower. But, perhaps crucially, the Rio bid also successfully communicated its messages about being committed to the social and economic transformations of a city derided for its inequalities and, second, for the way in which it advanced the argument that the Olympic Games should not only be the privilege of nations of the Global North. Moreover, there was evidence of significant public support for the Olympic bid. More crucially still was the clear willingness of government to sign up to financial guarantees to pay for the privilege of hosting the Olympic Games – commitments not made unconditionally by other contenders in the 2016 bid campaign.

In a study analysing media narratives of the 2016 bidding process, Carey, Mason & Misener (2011) found that the Rio bid team were successful at promoting these narratives, strengthening their bid in the process. They suggest that "the discourse surrounding the Rio de Janeiro bid put a greater focus on the capability of sport to reach out to disadvantaged populations and create balance within the global economy" (p.246). In their analysis of international media 'framing' Carey et al. (2011) also found that compared with their competitors in Tokyo, Chicago and Madrid, the Rio bid was viewed as an opportunity to address two main agendas: Sport for Development; and a North–South Divide. First, the carefully crafted vision of the Rio bid committee to use the Olympic Games to bring about – and accelerate – social and urban development to improve the conditions of those most in need was evident in media reporting and from the public pronouncements of political actors in the city, so that "the discourse surrounding the Rio de Janeiro bid focused on the human development nature of the bid and the social benefits of hosting the Olympic Games to the average Brazilian" (p.254). The development agenda was prescient as Darnell (2012) suggests that sporting mega events "are increasingly positioned as contributing to the sustainable achievement of development goals when hosted by emerging powers or low- and middle-income countries (LMICs)" (p.872). The Rio bid committee wanted to emphasise that a (relatively) poor country should be able to secure the rights to host the Olympic Games on the basis that it would lead to significant change to the social and economic fabric of the host city and, most importantly, its people. As Carey et al. (2011) suggest, media reporting of the Rio bid frequently included three key phrases related to development priorities – legacy, catalyst and transformation.

In terms of the second main narrative, the North–South divide, the Rio bid committee and its political supporters were also shrewd in the way they associated their bid with the IOC's UN-recognised commitment to use sport as a means to promote education, health, development, and peace (Carey et al., 2011). The Rio bid committee emphasised the 'right' of South America to host an Olympic Games in order to benefit from the unique opportunity presented by this sporting mega event to improve physical sporting infrastructures, alongside increasing employment and developing the business and private sector. Rio emphasised the scholarship narrative detailed in Chapter 5, and it was also able to make the case that it had the necessary experience and expertise, accrued from its hosting of the 2007 Pan American Games. President Lula da Silva was particularly prominent in espousing the narrative that a successful Rio bid would put South America on the Olympic map, further reinforcing "the symbolic nature of bringing the Olympic Games to a new territory" (Carey et al., 2011:255).

As discussed in Chapter 5, all prospective bidding cities and nations compete against each other, whilst also trying to influence the awarding body. In the case of the race for the 2016 Olympic Games, the IOC had faced significant criticism for its decision to award the 2008 Olympic Games to Beijing. It was facing ongoing pressure to reform and to stay true to the principles and values of the Olympic Movement in its criteria for awarding the Olympic Games. Rio's bid narrative and campaigning tactics sought to convince the IOC that awarding the rights to the Brazilian city would benefit it as much as the host itself. The Sport for Development agenda, the focus on transforming the lives of the most marginalised and the unconditional support of all three levels of government were designed to assuage concerns about the Rio bid in the eyes of the awarding body.

Technical dimensions: urban transformations

A key feature of sporting mega event bidding is that a successful candidature leads to a contractually binding partnership with the awarding body that will commit the host to deliver infrastructural, legislative and commercial conditions (Lauermann, 2017). Interestingly, for the Rio 2016 bid, the city was able to fall back on previous successful bids to highlight that these promises had been delivered, especially in the development of "areas of excellence" (Curi, Knijnik & Mascarenhas, 2011:144) that would be viewed positively by the IOC in the presentation of the Olympics to watching audiences. Moreover, having failed to secure the rights to host the 2012 Olympic Games, Rio's bid committee was acutely aware of the need to produce a sound technical bid to convince the IOC of its capacity and capability to host. As Michael Payne, Broadcast Director with the bid committee suggested, "no amount of emotion of political sympathy was going to carry the day, if the fundamental proposition was not sound" (Payne, 2009 [online]).

As discussed previously, the Rio bid was successful in communicating its hope that the Games would enable the city to address its systemic human and social development problems. The IOC was impressed by Rio's commitment to use the Games as a lever to address the social and economic inequality experienced by many of the city's residents, particularly those living in the (in)famous favelas. One of the key features of Rio's bid was the identification of priority development areas in the city – promoted as being of benefit for all. However, in reality, several critics point to the additional investment in areas already in receipt of significant levels of public investment – such as the Barra da Tijuca area (Gaffney, 2015).

The Olympic bid also provided the basis for Rio's political and economic elite to initiate and advance other developments that may not have happened had the bid not been successful. For example, the port revitalisation project at Porto Maravilha received support on the back of Rio's successful candidacy as the authorities lobbied to ensure some Olympic venues and associated facilities (e.g. media village) were located in this area. As Broudehoux & Sánchez (2015:114) suggest, "by establishing Porto Maravilha as one of the great Olympic legacies to the city, authorities managed to capitalize upon its association with the Olympic brand to help market the real estate project". One of the problematics associated with event bidding processes is the perception that the bid book put together by the bid committee and 'guaranteed' by various levels of government will actually be materialised once the rights to host the event are awarded. In Rio, the bid book contained an ambitious commitment to clean up 80% of Guanabara Bay, an area of water that had suffered from raw sewage and stormwater flowing into it from Rio's favelas. Despite these sorts of commitments being an important element of the 'sustainability' pillar of the technical requirements for potential Games hosts, Gaffney (2016 [online]) suggests that this bid commitment was not met because "neither would take any responsibility for the completion of the project. The City always said it was a State responsibility and the IOC said that it was a promise of the bid committee". That said, in terms of successful event bids, the support of three levels of government was viewed as crucial to Rio's success. The Federal Government had to approve sixty-four guarantees to meet the operational and logistical needs of the Games, including those relating to the dispensation of visa requirements, transport and traffic commitments and legacy projects relating to infrastructure and crucially the revitalisation of the port area.

In its bid, Rio made the case that four main urban areas would benefit evenly from the proposed urban developments. This commitment aligned with the bid narrative, with social and economic development at its heart, but in reality, some of the areas were already relatively affluent. To 'guarantee' a safe Games, with a carnival-like experience for visitors, athletes, and sponsors alike, Rio's bid team needed to emphasise the compact nature of the Games experience, whilst also carefully fitting these plans in with a wider urban masterplan that sought to 'develop' key priority area for future investment and consumption activity. Though the rhetoric of the bid contained reference to transformation of the urban environment for all, in reality the technical plan had to ensure that the city's less salubrious sectors were either 'developed' or made less visible (Steinbrink, 2013).

Campaign tactics and lobbying: the charm offensive

Crucial to Rio's ultimate success in the bidding process was the alliance formed between political actors across the three levels of government. At the national level,

President Lula played a significant external role in the bid process, emphasising Brazil's economic success and drawing attention (to the IOC) throughout that the Olympic Games had never been held in South America – a blot on the Olympic Movement (see Chapter 8).

Rio's successful bid for the rights to host the 2016 Olympic Games was in large part due to the successful communication of its principal bid narratives and the sophistication of the campaigning and lobbying tactics it utilised. Evidencing clear political support (and financial guarantees) has become more important for the IOC as it assesses prospective candidate cities, and Rio was particularly strong in that regard. From the bid book, through presentations at SportAccord, to the final presentation in Copenhagen, the Rio bid committee wasted no opportunity to emphasise support at every level of government. Payne (2009) called the President, the Governor or Rio and the Mayor the 'dream team' set of politicians, and they were each active in campaigning in a fashion not matched by their competitors.

As discussed briefly in Chapter 7, President Lula da Silva was a very prominent figure throughout the bid process, demonstrating powerful personal and political commitment to the bid. Though Rio won the bidding contest easily in the end (by over 30 votes), President de Silva's interventions were crucial in making an emotive, yet substantive case, that convinced voting IOC delegates. In his final speech to the delegates in Copenhagen, da Silva reinforced the prominent, development-focused narrative that had dominated the bid. He suggested that "the opportunity now is to expand the Games to new continents…send a powerful message to the world that the Olympic Games belong to all people, all continents, and to all humanity" (Gibson, 2009 [online]). President Lula's presence at Copenhagen was the culmination of nearly two years of carefully planned public appearances and participation in IOC delegations that provided Rio with an advantage over its competitors in the run up to the vote. As Payne (2009) contends:

> President Lula did not just come to the IOC Evaluation Commission once, but three times. He did not just write a general letter to the IOC membership, but wrote 110 individual, personal letters and had his Ambassadors deliver them by hand. Lula made a point of extending his stay in London after the G20 meetings, to go out to the Olympic Park and meet with Olympic officials.

Though President Obama and his wife Michelle flew into Copenhagen to make last-minute impassioned pleas to award the Games to Chicago, it fell on deaf ears, mainly because of doubts over the financial guarantees not being as watertight as those provided by the Brazilian delegation. Moreover, there was a sense that the IOC had got to know President Lula and the other elected officials well over the preceding months and that, alongside the strong 'transformational' narrative, ultimately proved successful. As discussed in Chapter 6, the support of political leaders or other influential ambassadors can prove decisive when the bidding contest is tight. Notably, the Rio 2016 bid committee was populated with people well known to the IOC or within the wider Olympic Movement, especially its leader who was a well-respected IOC member.

Moreover, an increasingly prominent feature of all major sporting events bids is the appointment of a team of specialist bid advisors, with international experience to ensure the bid campaign strikes a chord with the right audience(s). The Rio 2016 bid appointed experts in the technical area (Craig McLatchey, Sydney 2000), communications (Mike Lee, London 2012), presentations (Scott Givens, Salt Lake City), international relations (Francoise Zweifel), and broadcast (Michael Payne, former IOC Marketing). These experts informed the bid committee chair, Nuzman, and the three levels of government so important to the Rio bid case. Payne (2009) suggests that Rio, compared with its competitors, was more effective in realising that a sound technical bid was just the start – rather than the end – of the process. In its presentations and inspection visits, the Rio bid committee sought to address the bigger question of how a successful bid would help the IOC achieve its ambitions. It did this by emphasising why it 'needed' to host the Games (to lever change in the city, country and continent), its economic strength as a country during a time of global financial recession and, perhaps most crucially, by fore-grounding the sentimental dimension of South America not having previously hosted the Olympic Games. On the financial side, the Rio bid committee brought in the Governor of the Central Bank of Brazil to emphasise the strength of the Brazilian economy to cope with the global financial downturn, providing the 'gravitas' (Payne, 2009) to allay the IOCs fears – something its principal competitor, Chicago, never managed to replicate. On the international stage, Payne (2009) again suggested that the idea of showing a map of the world to illustrate the absence of South America was a political masterstroke. It provided a simple but effective means of tugging at the IOC members' consciences – especially as they were able to quantify that the other candidates came from continents that had previously hosted multiple Summer and Winter Olympic Games (e.g. Europe thirty, Asia five and North America ten).

The Rio bid committee also used a range of other tactics in the build up to the vote in Copenhagen, especially around the communications strategy designed and implemented by Mike Lee, who had been instrumental in London's successful bid campaign for the 2012 Olympic Games. The Rio bid used its media expertise to successfully promote its technical and financial strength alongside a powerful emotional appeal that ultimately convinced IOC members that it was a 'head' and a 'heart' decision to award the Games to the city. Before the inspection visit, this media work provided the necessary platform to then convince the IOC Evaluation Commission itself – where again subtle tactics were deployed. First, bid organisers chose 1 May as the day the inspectors would be toured around the city's venues because it was a holiday in Brazil – meaning that traffic congestion would be less noticeable. Second, they encouraged Rio's residents to dress in the colours of the country – green and yellow – and fly the national flag on that day of celebration to highlight 'spontaneous' public support for the bid (GamesBids, 2009). Third, the organisers left no stone unturned in preparing to host the Evaluation Commission, with two dress rehearsals organised to ensure each level of government and the sport federations provided consistent and coherent responses to questions. Payne (2009) describes how a team of experts were flown in from across the world to question the bid team about their plans. Ultimately, the Rio bid team made a positive impression on the IOC Evaluation Commission, which provided a glowing assessment of the bid in the report submitted to IOC members before the final vote. Tactically, the IOC Evaluation Commission visit represented an important 'moment' for Rio as it strengthened its position in the race, whereas other candidates were unable to allay ongoing doubts about the level of support around financial commitments (e.g. Chicago). Whereas Rio's principal stakeholders exuded unity and togetherness, with clear commitments to the financial terms set by the IOC, the Chicago bid experienced inconsistent support from the United States Olympic Committee and, internally, from its own City Council.

It was the small touches that operationalised Rio's more coherent vision for the Games, illustrated in the final presentation to IOC members being delivered in four languages. This apparently small gesture was indicative of a clear strategy for marketing its bid to the core electorate – IOC members. Compared with its rivals, the Rio bid team was much more successful at understanding the interests and concerns of each IOC member than its competitors. As Payne (2009) suggests, from inside the bid machine, detailed attention was paid to building relationships with IOC members during formal visits and presentations, and as part of Brazilian diplomatic efforts more generally. Though Rio was successful at communicating what hosting an Olympic Games would mean for the city, the region and the nation, it also emphasised how awarding the Games would benefit the Olympic Movement. Given how precarious and under scrutiny the IOC and the Olympic Movement had been before and after the Beijing Olympics, this was an intelligent strategy. In 2009, the Olympic Movement needed Rio as much as Rio needed the Olympics. Clift & Andrews (2012) reinforce this view, arguing that the IOC voting members "were cognisant of Brazil's increasingly prominent position on the global economic (and thereby political) stage: a position and influence from which the Olympic Movement could doubtless seek to capitalise" (p.211).

Resistance and alternative campaigns: silent voices

It is not possible to talk of opposition to the 2016 Olympic Games bid without acknowledging the extent of resistance evident for preceding sporting mega event bids. In fact, Broudehoux & Sánchez (2015) argue that "many of the resistance groups born during the Pan American Games, such as the Comitê Social do Pan (Social Committee for the Panamerican Games)…morphed into organizations fighting the Olympics and the World Cup" (p.112).

In the preceding chapter, we discussed the way in which bid committees and their supporters seek to secure the participation and support of all, a public relations exercise designed to divert attention from 'material', local concerns and to provide the external awarding body (the IOC) with evidence of public support. In this spirit of togetherness, successfully crafted by the Rio bid committee, opposing the bid can be perceived as unpatriotic or stunting the future economic and social prospects of a city. One of the principal strategies adopted by organisers is to incorporate popular political leaders, celebrities, and minority groups to back the bid, neutralising opposition in the process. When organisers steal a march on oppositional groups and interests, it can then be difficult to secure traction in the media for their oppositional messages (Pavoni, 2015), whatever their merit. Gaffney (2013) stresses that mega event planning processes, which he views negatively, begin far in advance of host selection and involve external agents looking to benefit from the urban developments that are enshrined within bid books. He goes on to suggest that:

> these coalitions create bid dossiers that are attuned to the interests of stakeholders. While this would ideally include civil society groups, even in consolidated democracies such as Canada (Vancouver 2010) and Great Britain (London 2012), civil society groups are grossly underrepresented in the planning stages.
>
> *(p.3929)*

These planning stages include the bid process itself, where there has been "lack of public stakeholder participation in the formulation of the bid document" (p.3930). The Olympic Plan, which committed Rio to significant public expenditure and urban development initiatives largely bypassed democratic decision-making (Saborio, 2013). Saborio (2013) further emphasises how bids for the FIFA World Cup and the Olympic Games sought to "delegitimize political protests" (p.135), particularly through the pacification processes that were introduced in 2008 after Brazil had secured the right to host the 2014 FIFA World Cup and in advance of being awarded the 2016 Olympic Games.

At one level, sporting mega events such as the Rio 2016 Olympic Games are intended to "generate a de-politicized atmosphere of consensus, enjoyment and entertainment, from which any political disturbance must be eliminated" (Pavoni, 2015:6). In this sense political tension is to be neutralised and threats pacified. Lauermann (2017) has suggested the timelines required for events planning, including bidding, make democratic displacement a real problem for social movements and other segments of civil society, especially when they hope to halt Olympic-related urban plans. But Lauermann (2017) suggests that protest tends to be reactive, overly localised and context specific rather than proactive and focused on the generalised problems with mega events, "the core institutional inequalities which produce those impacts are designed earlier during the bid phase" (Lauermann, 2017:217). Also, drawing on Boykoff (2014), he suggests the moment of movements' effect is problematic as it is temporary and often too late to alter well-embedded plans. Looking at the absence of extensive protest activity around the bidding process for the 2016 Olympic Games, it looks as though the organiser's strategy was effective – especially in the way it sought to engage the city's public with the idea of Rio (and South America) deserving to win the rights to the host the Olympic Games for the first time, and the social and economic transformation that hosting would bring.

In his blog documenting Rio's change from hosting the 2007 Pan American Games through to the Rio 2016 Olympics, Chris Gaffney provides useful insights into the extent of organisation and mobilisation that took place in the city around the Olympic bid. In an interview posted just after the IOC awarded the rights to the host the Olympics to Rio, he states:

> the people in the communities are trying to organize. There's a lot of co-option that goes on of course, clientist politics in Brazil are very much still alive and well, and then the hegemony of the media outlets prevents the story from getting out there. The forces allied in favor of the Olympics are quite strong and those against it almost nil. There are social groups organizing but they have very little coverage in the general media.
>
> *(Gaffney, 2009 [online])*

Not long after this post was published, there was evidence of immediate Olympic-related opposition, once residents of the city became aware of the legislative changes required on the award of the Games and the subsequent announcement of planned evictions that had not been expected so soon after the excitement and elation associated with the IOC announcement. What becomes clear about the apparent absence of coordinated opposition to the Rio 2016 Olympic bid itself is that the bid committee was successful at neutralising resistance and pacifying threats to the successful marketing of a unified political and sporting effort. Rio's experienced bid team stole a march – as bid teams often do – on social movements concerned about the urban development vision facilitated by mega event planning, and crafted a strategy to secure popular support that was translated into visible participation for important moments in the Olympic bid phase. For example, the IOC Evaluation Commission visit was choreographed so that Rio's 'colourful' cariocas were emblazoned with the colours of the Brazilian flag to demonstrate support for the bid. Though post-award, both the city of Rio and the Brazilian nation have been the site of extensive 'popular' protests centred on the excesses of sporting mega events, pre-bid these expressions of opposition were less visible or effective at influencing the shape of the urban developments that ensued. Given the political, economic and social crises that Rio, and the Brazilian nation, have experienced since 2009, it is safe to assume that the 'politics were too late' – that coordinated opposition to the very idea of hosting the Olympic Games was not present from 2007 to 2009.

Conclusions

In this chapter we have discussed how the bidding process for the rights to host the 2016 Olympic Games is illustrative of the main arguments advanced in this book. First, we have shown how the Rio bid originated from a desire in Rio (and Brazil more generally) to use mega events as a vehicle of urban development. The city had already committed to these events being part of a strategic development strategy designed to attract mobile capital through improving the city's image, generating greater external investment and global recognition. The Olympic bid fitted neatly into this plan, building on the successful 2014 FIFA World Cup bid, in which Rio was to be one of the host cities. However, as the discussion has shown, having a strategic ambition to bid is unlikely to be sufficient to persuade the powerful awarding body that its precious asset will be safe in your hands. Rio established a very experienced and well connected bid team and then devised a ten-point strategy (Payne, 2009) that sought to position its bid as financially, technically and emotionally strong. The bid committee's tactical nous enabled it to out-manoeuvre its main competitors, taking it from an outsider at the outset of the bid contest, to the eventual winner within a relatively short period of time. Its unified political (and popular) support impressed the key IOC influencers and it was tactually astute, exploiting every opportunity to remind voting members that the Olympic Games had never been hosted in South America. It also managed a public relations campaign, internally and externally, that quelled internal dissent to the point that there was little visible opposition to threaten the carefully crafted impression management. Rio's bid provides an exemplar of the importance of narrative and persuasion in a successful campaign. It convinced the IOC that the city could deliver a technically proficient, and financially lucrative Games, whilst also providing the Olympic Movement with a vision for its own future. At the same time, it offered the citizens of Rio the prospect of being the first South American Olympic host, alongside material improvements to the city's transport infrastructures, housing, sport facilities and global standing.

References

Boykoff, J. (2014) *Celebration capitalism and the Olympic Games.* London: Routledge.

Broudehoux, A-M. and Sánchez, F. (2015) The politics of mega event planning in Rio de Janeiro: Contesting the Olympic City of Exception. In V. Viehoff and G. Poynter (eds), *Mega-event cities: Urban legacies of global sports events* (pp.109–122). London: Routledge.

Carey, M., Mason, D.S. and Misener, L. (2011) Social responsibility and the competitive bid process for major sporting events. *Journal of Sport & Social Issues*, 35(3), pp.246–263.

Clift, B.C. and Andrews, D.L. (2012) Living Lula's passion?: The politics of Rio 2016. In H. Lenskyj and S. Wagg (eds), *The Palgrave Handbook of Olympic Studies* (pp.210–229). London: Palgrave Macmillan.

Curi, M., Knijnik, J. and Mascarenhas, G. (2011) The Pan American Games in Rio de Janeiro 2007: Consequences of a sport mega-event on a BRIC country. *International Review for the Sociology of Sport*, 46(2), pp.140–156.

Darnell, S.C. (2012) *Olympism in Action*, Olympic hosting and the politics of 'Sport for Development and Peace': Investigating the development discourses of Rio 2016. *Sport in Society*, 15(6), pp.869–887.

Gaffney, C. (2009) Interview with Al Jazeera. Available at http://geostadia.blogspot.co.uk/2009/12/interview-with-al-jazeera.html (accessed 23 February 2017).

Gaffney, C. (2013) Between discourse and reality: The un-sustainability of mega-event planning. *Sustainability*, 5(9), pp.3926–3940.

Gaffney, C. (2015) Gentrifications in pre-Olympic Rio de Janeiro. *Urban Geography*, 37(8), pp.1132–1153.

Gaffney, C. (2016) A long and short goodbye to the country of the eternal present. Available at http://geostadia.blogspot.co.uk/2016/09/a-long-and-short-goodbye-to-country-of.html (accessed 6 February 2017).

GamesBids (2009) Rio 2016 Awaits IOC Commission. Available at http://gamesbids.com/eng/summer-olympic-bids/rio-2016/rio-2016-awaits-ioc-commission/ (accessed 6 February 2017).

Gibson, O. (2009) Olympics 2016: Tearful Pele and weeping Lula greet historic win for Rio. https://www.theguardian.com/sport/2009/oct/02/olympics-2016-games-rio-pele (accessed 2 February 2017).

Lauermann, J. (2017) Politics as early as possible: Democratizing the Olympics by contesting Olympic bids. In C. Colomb and J. Novy (eds), *Protest and resistance in the tourist city*. London: Routledge.

Pavoni, A. (2015) Resistant legacies. *Annals of Leisure Research*, 18(4), pp.470–490.

Payne, M. (2009) The race for 2016 – How Rio won. Available at http://www.michaelrpayne.com/how_rio_won.html (accessed 6 February 2017).

Saborio, S. (2013) The pacification of the favelas: mega events, global competitiveness, and the neutralization of marginality. *Socialist Studies*, pp.130–145.

Steinbrink, M. (2013) Festi*favel*isation: Mega events, slums and strategic city-staging – the example of Rio de Janeiro. *Die Erde*, 144(2), pp.129–145.

10

MARSEILLE-PROVENCE 2013

'The unquenchable thirst for creative destruction'

Introduction

The French city of Marseille and its successful bid to become 2013 European Capital of Culture, incorporating both the city and the wider surrounding region of Marseille-Provence, offers interesting insights into a number of the issues discussed throughout this book. The city is, in many ways, representative of many former industrial cities which have sought to place culture and bidding for cultural events at the heart of their regeneration strategies. The story of Marseille-Provence's bid demonstrates clearly how successful bids are typically constructed and communicated, but also highlights the subjective reality of the bidding process where claims advanced in the bidding process on behalf of prospective hosts do not necessarily reflect the lived reality of that locale. The Marseille-Provence 2013 case also provides insights into the governance and management of urban spaces, the role of peripatetic event bids in the development strategies of cities and the long-term implications for the destination. Each of these issues is examined over the course of this chapter. We begin by providing background context to the European Capital of Culture competition itself before moving on to explain the motivations underpinning Marseille-Provence's desire to bid for the title. We then discuss how Marseille-Provence's bid demonstrated several technical strengths which were exploited to impress the judging panel and how it constructed a powerful narrative of poly-ethnism and multi-culturalism that contributed significantly to its ultimate success.

We also consider to what extent the construction of a powerful storyline for the Marseille-Provence bid was just that; a carefully constructed mythology that gave an air of cosmopolitanism and cultural participation which perhaps did not exist to the extent articulated in the bidding documentation. Finally, we also critique the extent to which the promises and plans detailed in the bidding documentation actually bore resemblance to what occurred with Marseille, and the wider Provence region in the lead up to, and immediate aftermath of, the year of culture celebrations. Here we highlight that, whilst well-constructed, polished and successful, the Marseille-Provence 2013 European Capital of Culture bid is, in essence, a textbook example of how to bid, but by being so it is also open to several of the critiques we have made elsewhere in this book.

European Capital of Culture: a brief overview

The European Capital of Culture (ECoC) programme (formerly European City of Culture) is the flagship cultural initiative of the European Union (European Commission, 2014). The award enables a European city to host a year-long cultural programme under the banner of being a Capital of Culture for a named year. Starting in 1985, with the inaugural celebration in Athens, the event has evolved significantly in the subsequent 32 years. Initially, the award represented a celebration of the pinnacle of European cultural activity and centred around a celebration of the arts within the host locale. Early awards centred around historically significant European cultural hubs such as Athens (1985), Florence (1986), Amsterdam (1987), Berlin (1988) and Paris (1989). However, beginning with Glasgow in 1990 (as discussed in Chapter 2), the award has become more focused on the contribution the title can make to the economic, physical and social redevelopment and regeneration of the host city (or region). Increasingly, the award is viewed as "a catalyst for a step-change in the city" (European Commission, 2014:4) with the celebration expected to deliver an increase in civic pride, cultural participation, the invigoration of the host's cultural offer and an increased profile resulting in greater tourism inflows, bringing economic rewards. This change in emphasis is reflected in the profile of successful hosts, with more recent iterations of the event being awarded to cities intending to use the award as a catalyst for redevelopment, including Rotterdam (2001), Liverpool (2008) and Maribor (2012). In addition, as the European Union itself has grown in membership so too has the scope of the ECoC, and since the 2000 iteration, which saw nine cities named as cultural capitals to celebrate the new millennium, the award has typically been made to two cities from separate member states, simultaneously. The award is now rotated amongst member states, with cities within the scheduled nation competing for the right to host that given year's celebration. From 2021, each third year will see the appointment of another Capital of Culture chosen from an open selection process across all member states. In total, from 1985 to 2017, there have been 56 European Capitals of Culture to date (European Commission, 2017 [online]).

The bid process for the award is typical of most peripatetic events, as detailed in Chapter 4. Candidate cities in the scheduled hosting nation typically begin the bid process six years prior to the year of celebration itself. Any city within the nation may bid and can choose to involve a wider region surrounding the municipality. Candidate cities must demonstrate a "forward-looking programme", which goes beyond the normal cultural activity of the city and can be considered as "not business as usual" (European Commission, 2014:7). In addition, the programme must be European in scope and "highlight both the common features and the diversity of cultures in Europe", representing a long-term commitment to a project which requires "6–7 years of sustained, continual effort" (ibid.). The final award, made by a panel of independent experts over the course of a two stage application process and centred around an application form (or bid book) of approximately 80–100 pages, is based upon six key criteria: 'contribution to the long-term cultural strategy'; 'European dimension'; 'cultural and artistic content'; 'capacity to deliver'; 'outreach'; and 'management'. Here, a number of themes discussed previously in this text come to the fore. Requirements around notions of 'capacity to deliver' and 'management' fit comfortably with the technical requirements discussed in Chapter 4, and reflect the need for awarding bodies to ascertain the ability of a potential host to successfully deliver the event if chosen. Areas such as 'outreach' reflect the growing legacy requirements of bids, detailing the transformative power of the event upon the host locale and ensuring the award acts as more than an extravagant travelling circus, consuming resources and leaving nothing behind (as detailed in Chapter 7). However, the criteria around the need to be 'European' and to promote "European integration and current European themes" (European Commission, 2014:9), also highlight the way in which the awarding body reinforces its priorities and strategic agendas through the award. In the case of the ECoC, the promotion, sustention and legitimation of the notion of a pan-European cultural identity is evident, reinforcing the need for a pan-European governmental body such as the European Union.

Marseille-Provence 2013: rationale for bidding

In 2008, Marseille-Provence was selected ahead of Toulouse, Lyon and Bordeaux as the French representative for the 2013 ECoC award, allowing the city to share hosting rights with Kosice (Slovakia) for the year. The Marseille-Provence bid was heralded as the last link in a thirty-year regeneration chain (Andres, 2011), completing the city's journey from its post-industrial decline in the 1960s through to the 1980s and allowing the city to once again take its place as a major cultural hub within France. In many ways, the experience of Marseille is similar to that of several other European and other first world cities in the global age, particularly former industrial ports. Located on the south coast of France, Marseille has a long history as a busy port, tracing its heritage back over 1,500 years. The city served as France's leading Mediterranean military port during the eighteenth century and, as rapid industrialisation took place across Europe, the city became a hub of manufacturing and trade. However, as Andres (2013) and Bullen (2011) highlight, the post-industrial decline of these industries caused significant problems for the city and, by the 1980s, Marseille was blighted by high unemployment, population decline, a political and social crisis and racial tensions exacerbated by the success of far-right extremist political parties. As with several of the other cities discussed elsewhere in this book (see the discussion on Glasgow in Chapter 3, for example), the local authority for the region turned to the cultural and creative industries as a means of reversing the city's fortunes (Andres & Chapain, 2013). Examining how Marseille achieved this highlights the ubiquity of development strategies across the world in relation to event bidding. First, it is notable that Marseille embraced the new urban entrepreneurialism (Harvey, 2002) which we have argued typifies many major cities. Evans (2011) highlights how the ECoC bid formed part of a longer-term, wider regeneration project within Marseille, aimed at rebuilding urban infrastructure, creating cultural spaces in the form of new facilities and growing the city-region's cultural bedrock in advance of the eventual bid itself. In Marseille, this took the form of the Euroméditerranée project which sought to rejuvenate a 480 hectare area surrounding the city's commercial harbour and Old Port (Euroméditerranée, 2010 [online]). The project, beginning in 1995, aimed to make Marseille one of the top 20 cities in Europe (ibid.) and reinforce its position as a Mediterranean hub (Andres, 2011). The first phase of the project (1995–2012) saw significant collaboration between local and national government and the European Union, centred around the development of urban space, transport networks and the consolidation or creation of venues and other cultural assets. Mimicking the activities of the private sector the Euroméditerranée project was overseen by a Board of Directors with day-to-day operations directed by a Chief Executive Officer. The organisation's role was similar to Garrett's (2004) view of contemporary governance, being more centred upon "enabling and empowering" (p.15) than directly controlling areas of activity. In the case of Euroméditerranée, project objectives highlighted a focus upon the need to "coordinate and guide partner actions" (Euroméditerranée, 2010) rather than direct action and highlighted an amorphous role in destination marketing and the strategic management of urban conglomerations, with little detail of how this happens in practice.

Moving on from this, in Chapters 4 and 7 we discussed the role and power given to non-elected bodies, operating at arm's length from elected officials but wielding significant influence over the shape of civic spaces and public finances. The second phase of the project (2013–2020) saw greater emphasis on the attraction of private sector funding, with a commitment to match each euro of public funding with four euros of private investment. However, this private investment was linked closely to the purchase of land redeveloped through public funding. Here, the redevelopment project could be seen to ape criticisms of mega event bidding and delivery, which Getz (2007:319) suggests enable "industry and the community's powerful elite [to] realise huge profits at the taxpayer's expense". In this situation, events are criticised as nothing more than a commercial 'land grab', securing prime locations for the commercial sector with the use of what is effectively public subsidy. Tellingly, the materials produced to outline the Euroméditerranée project have a promotional tone, emphasising €4 billion of public and private investment, the generation of 500,000 square metres of office and business spaces and 20,000 new jobs, and describe "a future where Marseille ranks among the most dynamic and influential cities in Europe" (Euroméditerranée, 2010:5). Place marketing discourses in particular are evident here. Perhaps inevitably, there have been significant criticisms of the project as a result. Andres (2011), whilst acknowledging successes in the economic terrain in terms of job creation and the transformation of the image of the city, highlights a lack of participation and engagement amongst the poorest members of the local community and questions the long-term, cohesive plan for the disparate projects forming the overall Euroméditerranée development. There is a clear sense that the project, whilst revitalising the destination brand of Marseille and creating a series of landmark properties and assets, has not necessarily led to profound transformation of the wider area or the populace.

Demonstrating technical competency

However, this development, whilst characteristic of the failings of many urban renewal projects, also acted as the catalyst for a successful Marseille-Provence bid. Indeed, Andres (2011) argues that the Euroméditerranée project was a condition *sine qua non* for the ECoC bid, demonstrating the city's commitment to its cultural regeneration and its ability to manage long-term cultural and infrastructure projects. In this sense, Marseille's Euroméditerranée project fits closely with our discussion in Chapter 4 surrounding the need to build a technical case to demonstrate to awarding bodies that a prospective host is capable of successfully delivering their event asset. In other chapters we have discussed Glasgow's hosting of smaller events in the lead up to the 2014 Commonwealth Games and Rio's use of the 2007 Pan-American Games as a staging point for a successful bid for the 2016 Olympic Games. Similarly, Euroméditerranée became the springboard to Marseille's successful bid for the 2013 ECoC award. The project enabled the city to articulate its bid within both the 'management' and 'capacity to deliver' dimensions of the bidding criteria outlined above, as well as demonstrating the required 'contribution to the long-term cultural strategy' of the region.

The project also enabled Marseille-Provence 2013 to evidence its ability to meet another key technical requirement of the bidding process we have discussed previously. In Chapter 4 we highlighted the importance of the composition of the bid committee as being integral to the success of any bid. Winning bids must demonstrate commitment from a wide range of stakeholders, particularly from the public sector. The Euroméditerranée project had already established this network in advance of the Marseille-Provence 2013 bid and, as Andres (2011) highlights, the Selection Panel awarding the title were assured of the strong political engagement of a wide range of municipal partners and support from the business community for the Capital of Culture bid. For Marseille-Provence a large number of these parties were already within the urban development tent as a result of the Euroméditerranée project and could be seen to be 'primed' for the next step in the evolution of the city – the almost inevitable bid for, ECoC. As Foley, McGillivray & McPherson (2012) highlight, broader urban development or regeneration projects create an inevitable movement and momentum within a locale. One project leads to a desire to bid for the 'next' step. One event creates the conditions both to demonstrate capacity to host the next, but also build the appetite to do so. Andres

(2011) identifies the ECoC as the inevitable result of the Euroméditerranée project which created venues in need of events to fill the latent capacity they create – a self-fulfilling prophecy of bidding.

The credibility created by the Euroméditerranée project was supplemented by a second decision which demonstrates Marseille-Provence 2013's suitability as a template for understanding other peripatetic event bids across the world – namely the appointment of a charismatic bid leader. In preceding chapters we have highlighted the importance of having leaders with expertise, experience and the ability to coordinate a bid process. These figures typically require the ability to establish and direct the complex networks of stakeholders around a bid, and rally the resources required to achieve success. In this case, the Marseille-Provence bid was exemplary, with Bernard Latarjet, a former advisor to President Mitterrand, being appointed to the role of Bid Director. As Andres (2011:65) suggested:

> Thanks to his networks and ability to neutrally and consensually discuss issues with all urban authorities, he managed to draw their attention. Moreover, his past experience gained him the respect of local cultural actors and artists as well as of local economic actors, confident in the serious nature of the application

Strong leadership, combined with the aforementioned track record of delivery and a raft of new facilities created by the Euroméditerranée project, provided Marseille-Provence with a strong technical foundation on which to base its bid, demonstrating the capability of the city as a potential host to the Selection Panel and maximising the likelihood of success. Ultimately, the Marseille-Provence bid was able to articulate a strong sense of both technical and professional capability. However, it also crafted a powerful narrative to underpin its bid, reinforcing the argument made in Chapter 5 that to be successful, potential hosts must go beyond demonstrating simple technical capability to articulate a 'story' to communicate the benefits of their candidacy over that of rivals.

'Welcoming the world': Marseille's bid narrative

In Chapter 5 we argued that successful event bids need to articulate a clear story as to why they should be chosen ahead of other candidates. We highlighted that such narratives must be located within the demands of the awarding body and in relation to the socio-political conditions of the bid cycle. We concluded that typically two narrative types; *scholarship* and *reward* dominate bid strategies. In the case of Marseille-Provence 2013, the bid team pursued a clear messaging campaign in line with a scholarship strategy.

To fully understand how this message developed and why it succeeded, it is worth briefly considering the socio-political context in which the ECoC award itself is located. As Staiger (2013) highlights, the early focus of the European Union was primarily economic. Indeed, trans-European collaboration, beginning in the aftermath of the Second World War, centred around the European Economic

Community and its efforts focussed upon cross-border market liberalisation rather than the creation of a single European identity or cultural community. Whilst culture emerged as an area of interest for the Community over the next twenty years, with a 'Document on European Identity' in Copenhagen in 1973 (Mittag, 2013), it was not until the establishment of the Maastricht Treaty in 1992 that a legal basis was formed for Community involvement with cultural matters (Staiger, 2013). In this setting, the ECoC award, initiated in the 1980s, can be seen as part of the increasing interest in social and cultural matters within the European Community and, subsequently, the European Union over the last thirty years. As the Union's purpose moved from economic integration to focussing on these social and cultural issues, initiatives such as the ECoC both promoted and legitimised European identity as a distinct entity. At its heart therefore, is a message of integration and multiculturalism. This is reflected in the bid criteria which emphasise:

> This is a European project. Programmes must highlight both the common features and the diversity of cultures in Europe. The overall vision of the event must be European and the programme must have an appeal at a European – and international – level.
>
> *(European Commission, 2014:7)*

It is in this context that the success of the Marseille-Provence 2013 bid can be understood. In addition to emphasising the strength of offer created by the Euro-méditerranée project, the Marseille-Provence bid focussed heavily on a narrative of integration and multi-culturalism which chimed strongly with the European Union's desire to communicate a pan-European identity. Throughout the bid documentation and campaign events held during the bid process a clear emphasis was placed on a range of key programme themes such as "Welcoming the World" and "Land of a Thousand Faces" (Embassy of France in London, 2013 [online]). These themes were designed to position Marseille-Provence as a multi-cultural region and locate it as the crossroads between Northern and Southern Europe and a gateway to Europe for the rest of the world. The Mediterranean identity of the city proved integral to the success of the bid (Ingram, 2009), allowing, as Latarjet explained, the Marseille-Provence bid to articulate clearly with European Union values of pan-European integration: "It is genuinely based on European cultural geopolitics. It gives priority to the Union's strategies and programmes to which Marseille-Provence can make the most efficient contributions" (Invest in Provence, unknown date [online]).

The Marseille-Provence bid also coalesced around wider geo-political issues relating to global migration and integration. Marseille's history as a port city and its close links to non-European countries, particularly those in nearby North African nations, was emphasised to present the Marseille-Provence bid as one not only of pan-European integration but a more global project. As discussed in Chapters 2 and 5, awarding bodies are often drawn to the symbolic politics of bids which offer an engagement with the social concerns of the period. In this case, Marseille-Provence, with its promise to celebrate the differing cultures of the 100+ communities and communes which make up the region, offered a timely opportunity for the Selection Panel to reward such globalism and gave the bid a unique selling point in the narrative stakes. This, combined with the classical scholarship narrative of helping to rejuvenate a city laid low by post-industrial decline through the use of the creative and cultural industries, provided Marseille-Provence 2013 with a story which was clearly attuned to the need – both explicit and implicit – of the awarding body.

Critiquing Marseille: bid realities, bid by numbers and bidding fever

The Marseille-Provence 2013 bid represents an ideal case study for the many of the themes discussed throughout this book. The motivations underpinning the desire to bid and the location of the bid within the development strategy of the city are typical of many other cities and nations around the world. Evans (2011) draws parallels between Rotterdam and Marseille, seeing them both as indicative of the incremental regeneration common to other port cities. Andres & Chapain (2013) link the city to Birmingham, holding both as examples of 'second cities' using their creative industries to drive regeneration. The comparisons extend beyond Europe, with Van Dyck (2010) highlighting similarities between Marseille's cultural redevelopment and that of Montreal, Canada. In addition, the composition of the bid team demonstrates the approach taken by many other cities, building consent across a political and business spectrum, under the leadership of a strong figurehead and, as the previous section detailed, the narrative of scholarship and development matches so many other post-industrial cities. However, whilst the bid may be a fine example of many of the successful approaches we have discussed here, and indeed it is referenced by the European Commission (2014) in their advice to bidding cities, it is also typical of one of the key concerns raised earlier in this text. In Chapter 4 we argued that the use of peripatetic 'bid gurus', who travel from one nation to another, could potentially lead to homogenous bids which differ little from one another in real terms. Reviewing the case of Marseille-Provence 2013, it is difficult to isolate a unique proposition, something about the bid which distinguishes it from the herd of other cities and nations seeking to secure hosting rights to a major sporting or cultural event. Indeed, just as one report criticised Marseille's redeveloped harbour and the cultural venues which now dominate it as a "spasm of accelerated projects, favouring exterior image and the power of spectacle over long-term, joined up thinking" (*The Guardian*, 2013 [online]), so too can the bid itself be criticised as being formulaic and 'by the numbers'. Previously, we have drawn upon criticism by Foley et al. (2012) of development strategies which rely on elite and folkloric cultural forms at the expense of more representative forms of activity. Here we can link this notion to a bidding 'formula' which combines landmark cultural facilities, a coalition of bid representatives and an economic improvement plan dressed in the story-telling language of cultural inclusion and community development, but which says little about the reality of the bid candidate itself.

Andres' (2011) work can be seen to build on this further. She argues that the reality of the bid process can differ somewhat to the slick narratives produced by bid teams. Above we drew attention to the strength Marseille-Provence was able to highlight as a result of the diverse range of stakeholders who came together first for Euroméditerranée, and then for the ECoC bid, and how this cohesion became a key factor in the decision making process of the Selection Panel. However, whilst elements of the Euroméditerranée process *did* emerge from a long-term, sustained collaborative process, such as the development of the La Friche cultural complex (see Andres, 2013), the reality of these coalitions and partnerships around Marseille-Provence 2013 was more fraught and conflicted than outward appearances suggest. Bullen (2011) describes how political infighting continued to hinder progress and development within the metropolitan area in general and noted, in the case of the ECoC bid specifically, the withdrawal of Toulon from the project. Furthermore, Andres (2011) noted that the bid coalition was indeed more fragile, with Marseille dominating the relationship in practice, with the wider region included, only notionally, as an equal partner in the bid process. The outward appearance of the bid, as a polished collaborative effort, bore little resemblance to the actual reality of the process. Bullen draws upon Erik Swyndegouw's words to highlight that "the production of new social spatial scales remains a deeply conflicted process" (cited in Bullen, 2011:3).

Similarly, the narrative employed by the bid team is open to critique and contestation. As discussed previously, Marseille-Provence made use of a scholarship narrative which relied heavily on the themes of multi-culturalism and development. As Bullen's (2011) work suggests, Marseille-Provence 2013's bid followed in the footsteps of other cities, including Glasgow and Liverpool, and positioned the ECoC award as a gateway to a brighter future, part of a broader cultural metropolitan project. However, whilst themes such as 'Welcoming the World' and 'Land of a Thousand Faces' made for a powerful narrative, it is possible to cast doubts on the extent to which this accurately reflected the reality of the bid. First, Andres (2011) suggests the poly-ethnic image of Marseille is a myth, with other French cities, such as Paris and Lyon, having a stronger case to be seen as the nation's multi-cultural hub, boasting populations more diverse. Further, there is a case to suggest a disconnect between the iconic venues and flagship cultural complexes built to showcase the culture of Marseille-Provence and the communities surrounding them. Andres (2011) emphasised, ahead of the year of culture, the need to ensure the ECoC event did not become segregationist and disconnected from local needs, but by 2013 there were questions raised (*The Guardian*, 2013) regarding the actual contribution the ECoC celebrations were making to the lived experience of the impoverished communities surrounding these flagship buildings. This fits with the criticism of previous hosts of the ECoC award by the likes of Jones & Wilks-Heeg (2004), who have highlighted a prioritisation of tourists over residents and local cultures. Bullen (2011:3) highlights that "considerable interrogation about whether these networks and collaboration would last after the fireworks had exploded on the eve of 2014"; particularly with concerns regarding the sustainability of long-term funding for initiatives designed to foster cultural participation, there is a danger that flagship facilities become oases of elitism leaving improvised communities with their faces pressed against the glass, locals paying for others to play. In this sense, there is a disconnect between the narratives used to sell a bid and ensure it is successful and what happens in practice thereafter.

These two points combine to highlight a danger of 'by the numbers' bidding. The narrative of harmonious partnerships and grand redevelopment programmes developed by Marseille-Provence could be located anywhere and nowhere, simultaneously. The complexities and inconsistencies of place are smoothed and polished into empty statements which become problematic to then actualise within the place itself. In this setting, it becomes clear why many potential hosts increasingly face challenges, as we have seen elsewhere in this book (see Chapter 8), from oppositional movements which are increasingly sceptical of this 'marketing brochure' approach to bidding and seek answers to how securing event hosting rights will actually benefit the host in the long term.

Finally, Marseille-Provence 2013 allows us to build on this scepticism further and ask questions about the long-term contribution of bids to profound and sustained development within a host locale. As indicated at the outset of this chapter, the Marseille-Provence 2013 bid was positioned as the end of a long journey towards political, social and cultural transformation within the city and region. We have shown elsewhere in this book that this is often a powerful narrative, combining as it does, elements of both reward and scholarship narratives. However, rather than representing an end point in development, like many destinations, Marseille-Provence 2013 appears to have been the jumping off point for another, very different event bid, in this case the Marseille-Provence 2017 European Capital of Sport bid. This bid (see Marseille-Provence 2017 (2014)), submitted just months after the end of the year of culture celebrations, positioned the ECoC award as a step on the journey towards becoming the European Capital of Sport. Just as the 2013 bid team used the Euroméditerranée project as evidence to support the ECoC bid, the 2017 bid team repositioned the ECoC award as evidence of the city's ability to deliver a bigger event. In addition, the European Capital of Sport team drew heavily on the language of the ECoC bid, talking again of a multi-cultural city and a predisposition towards strategic teamworking as a unique strength, and also the need for the 'reinvention' of the city, but with sport replacing culture as the vehicle of change in this instance. Moving from culture to sport so quickly and using the same development language to underpin a new bid raises concerns regarding the long-term sustainability of the ECoC bid. If it were truly successful, would the city really *need* to bid for an alternative award so soon after the first celebration? If it were truly sustainable, would the city be moving away from its focus on culture to pursue sporting prominence so quickly? The answer to this can be found in the discussion by Foley et al. (2012) of event policy, where they argue that bidding has become an unreflexive response in many destinations. Bidding, indeed the general hosting of major events, has become reified with the value and contribution of events seemingly lacking interrogation. In such a world, bidding for the next event becomes an inevitability, with little reflection on the failures or successes of previous bids. Müller (2015, 2016) introduces an almost medical discourse into discussions around mega events, discussing 'mega event syndrome' and 'event seizure' to characterise the way in which such activity comes to dominate the development agenda of the host, infiltrating and overpowering other agendas. Black (2016) builds on this, introducing the language of addiction, referring to the mega event 'habit' and identifying some hosts, specifically in his case Calgary, as 'serial users' driven to bid for event after event in search of the next series of externalities and eventualities. Such habitual bidding brings to mind Bauman's (2000) characterisation of contemporary social life as being driven by an "over-whelming and ineradicable, unquenchable thirst for creative destruction (or of destructive creativity)" (p.28). Marseille-Provence, like many cities, regions and nations can be seen as being ensnared on the bidding treadmill, destined to search for new events for which to bid, cyclically moving from one award to another, suffering from, to continue the medicinal discourse, *bidding fever*.

Conclusion

This chapter has demonstrated how Marseille-Provence's bid to become 2013 European Capital of Culture can be seen as indicative of a range of bids from other destinations around the world for a wide range of peripatetic events. As we have demonstrated here, Marseille-Provence 2013 illustrates clearly a range of successful practices discussed throughout this book, particularly those covered in Part II. The approach taken to demonstrating both the technical and emotive elements of a bid campaign was, upon review, ideally placed to deliver a successful event bid. However, as we have also demonstrated, whilst ultimately successful, the Marseille-Provence 2013 bid, and its placement within the long-term development of the region, highlights a number of the challenges we have identified with bidding process in general. Given the disconnect between the images and narratives of the bid and the lived reality of Marseille-Provence's socio-political environment, the 2013 bid can be critiqued as a 'by-the-numbers' bid, typical of everywhere and nowhere simultaneously. At a wider level, the Marseille-Provence region, with its fast-changing bid priorities, raises questions regarding the extent to which decisions relating to why to bid and upon which event to focus are really considered in detail or as part of a long-term development plan. As we turn to our concluding thoughts on event bidding in the final chapter, the case of Marseille-Provence is perhaps most useful in that it returns our focus to a sentiment raised at the outset of this book: there is need to take a critical and reflexive view of the world of event bidding.

References

Andres, L. (2011) Alternative initiatives, cultural intermediaries and urban regeneration: The case of la Friche (Marseille). *European Planning Studies*, 19(5), pp.795–811.

Andres, L. (2013) Differential spaces, power hierarchy and collaborative planning: A critique of the role of temporary uses in shaping and making places. *Urban Studies*, 50(4), pp.759–775.

Andres, L. and Chapain, C. (2013) The integration of cultural and creative industries into local and regional development strategies in Birmingham and Marseille: Towards an inclusive and collaborative governance? *Regional Studies*, 47(2), pp.161–182.

Bauman, Z. (2000) *Liquid modernity*. Cambridge: Polity; Oxford: John Wiley & Sons.

Black, D.R. (2016) Managing the mega-event 'habit': Canada as serial user. *International Journal of Sport Policy & Politics*, pp.1–17.

Bullen, C. (2011) European Capital of Culture as regional development tool? The case of Marseilles-Provence 2013. *Tafter Journal*, p.42.

Embassy of France in London (2013) Marseille-Provance 2013 – European Capital of Culture Available at http://www.ambafrance-uk.org/Marseille-Provence-2013-European (accessed 18 March 2017).

European Commission (2014) European Capitals of Culture 2020–2033: Guide for cities preparing to bid. Available at https://ec.europa.eu/programmes/creative-europe/sites/ creative-europe/files/library/capitals-culture-candidates-guide_en.pdf (accessed 18 March 2017).

European Commission (2017) European Capitals of Culture more than 30 years. Available at https://ec.europa.eu/programmes/creative-europe/sites/creative-europe/files/library/ecoc-fact-sheet_en.pdf (accessed 18 March 2017).

Euroméditerranée (2010) The Euroméditerranée Marseille: Heartbeat of an historic Mediterranean city. Available at http://www.Euroméditerranée.fr/fileadmin/downloads/32pa gesanglais.pdf (accessed 18 March 2017).

Evans, G. (2011) Cities of Culture and the regeneration game. *London Journal of Tourism, Sport & Creative Industries*, 6, pp.5–18.

Foley, M., McGillivray, D. and McPherson, G. (2012) *Event policy: From theory to strategy*. London and New York: Routledge.

Garrett, R. (2004) The response of voluntary sports clubs to Sport England's Lottery funding: Cases of compliance, change and resistance. *Managing Leisure*, 9(1), pp.13–29.

Getz, D. (2007) *Event studies: Theory, research and policy for planned events*. London and New York: Routledge.

Harvey, D. (2002) From managerialism to entrepreneurialism: The transformation of urban governance in late capitalism. In G. Bridge, and S. Watson (eds), *The Blackwell city reader*. Oxford: Blackwell, pp.456–463.

Ingram, M. (2009) The artist and the city in "Euro-Mediterranean" Marseille: Redefining state cultural policy in an era of transnational governance. *City & Society*, 21(2), pp.268–292.

Invest in Provence (unknown date) Interview with Bernard Latarget. Available at http:// www.investinprovence.com/download/BERNARDLATARGETUK.pdf (accessed 18 March 2017).

Jones, P. and Wilks-Heeg, S. (2004) Capitalising culture: Liverpool 2008. *Local economy*, 19(4), pp.341–360.

Marseille-Provence 2017 (2014) Bid for the title of European Capital of Sport 2017. Available at http://www.aceseurope.eu/images/ACES/BIDFILES/marseillebidfile.pdf (accessed 18 March 2017).

Mittag, J. (2013) The changing concept of the European Capitals of Culture: Between the endorsement of European identity and city advertising. In K. Patel (ed.), *The cultural politics of Europe: European Capitals of Culture and European Union since the 1980s* (pp.39–54). London: Routledge.

Müller, M. (2015) The mega-event syndrome: Why so much goes wrong in mega-event planning and what to do about it. *Journal of the American Planning Association*, 81(1), pp.6–17.

Müller, M. (2016) How Mega-events capture their hosts: Event seizure and the World Cup 2018 in Russia. *Urban Geography*, pp.1–20.

Staiger, U. (2013) The European Capitals of Culture in context: Cultural policy and the European integration process. In K. Patel (ed.), *The cultural politics of Europe: European Capitals of Culture and European Union since the 1980s* (pp.19–38). London: Routledge.

The Guardian (2013) Marseille's £6bn Capital of Culture rebirth. Available at https://www.theguardian.com/artanddesign/2013/apr/01/marseille-capital-culture-architecture (accessed 18 March 2017).

Van Dyck, B. (2010) When the third sector builds the city. Brownfield transformation projects in Marseille and Montréal. Available at https://lirias.kuleuven.be/bitstream/123456789/290203/1/Final_When+the+third+sector+builds_17september.pdf (accessed 31 March 2017).

11

CONCLUSIONS

At the outset of this project we set out to fill a gap in the treatment of event bidding within the Academy, internationally. We argued that relatively little academic attention had been paid to a phenomenon that involves significant costs and generates a range of impacts on local, national and international constituencies. We approached the task with two main objectives in mind. First, we wanted to provide a theoretically informed text that considered the strategies and tactics used to develop event bids and looked beyond the generation of individual case studies only. We also wanted to furnish readers with theoretical perspectives that would enable them to develop a *critical commentary* on the bidding process itself and, crucially, on the struggles for power and influence that it represents. To that end, this book has unashamedly brought together theory and practice to help analyse the historical intersection between event bids and urban processes; assess power relations, conflicts, social inequalities and the unevenness of urban development approaches exemplified in event bids; and draw attention to marginalisations, exclusions and injustices (Brenner, 2009) in the event bidding process. In doing so, we have examined the prevailing rationales underpinning event bids, how they are turned into a coherent vision, how that vision is communicated to primary and secondary stakeholders and what strategies have been successful in securing bid success for cities and nations alike.

We have also drawn attention to a range of critical issues of growing significance in bidding contests, including concerns about suspect governance arrangements, corruption and impropriety, as well as the increasing prevalence, and success, of anti-bid protest and opposition movements in recent years. In the preceding ten chapters we have demonstrated that event bidding is much more than simply a sub-set of event management practice. Instead, event bidding is an important dimension in debates about competing versions of economic policy, urban policy, political leadership and populist campaigns, destination branding and place marketing. It involves public and private actors, legal and extra-legal activities, exceptional legislation and media persuasion. In this concluding chapter we return to the guiding research questions posited at the start of the book to illustrate our main contributions, before reflecting on the future of event bidding.

Event bidding: from motivation to persuasion

We have made it clear in this text that the rationales underpinning bidding processes are inseparable from the vagaries of neo-liberal economic systems. These drivers provide a force emanating from the necessity to bid as a mechanism to produce economic and cultural benefits to the host destination. However, we also argue strongly that the bid process itself is more illustrative of neo-liberal urban entrepreneurial processes than it would appear on first reading. Bids are not abstract entities but, instead, tie cities and nations into more permanent, material changes to legislation, urban planning and economic commitments, should they be successful. Bid processes enshrine exceptional measures on behalf of the state, although it is often a coalition of state and non-state actors that actually bid for sporting and cultural events. State actors subsidise bids that, if successful, often lead to significant alterations to urban planning, real estate purchase and retail environments. Bids do not happen by accident; they are the outcome of longer-term 'strategic planning' processes that locate major sporting and cultural events as a part of a choice development strategy (Broudehoux & Sánchez, 2015). Here, hosting events provides the host destination with a means of altering images, securing greater external investment, tourist visitation and global recognition. We argue that event bidding is a key component of the acceleration and intensification of urban entrepreneurial development because it provides a sense of urgency and temporal finitude to the process. Moreover, the event bidding process, especially for major and mega sporting events, further reinforces urban entrepreneurial discourses as awarding bodies require bidders to commit to significant urban transformations as a condition of their bid, including the suspension of established planning and legal regulations and the introduction of new norms to facilitate the exploitation of commercial opportunities for a range of investor interests. In essence, the bidding process allows unelected and unaccountable actors the ability to exert undue influence on local development policies in the name of submitting the strongest bid, facilitated by the state apparatus, to ensure the free flow and circulation of capital to sponsors and the like.

As we discussed in Chapter 2, even the nature of event bidding has changed over time, with the competition for peripatetic sporting events, in particular, experiencing both high and low points. We have shown how allegations of corruption and impropriety negatively affected interest in bidding for the Olympic Games in the late 1970s and early 1980s. However, the post-industrial urban restructuring that impacted on advanced liberal democracies of the West, in particular, in the ensuing period re-energised the bidding competition as prospective hosts sought to use major sport and cultural events as a vehicle for economic, cultural and social change. Over the last two decades event bidding has become even more important as a choice development strategy, especially for second tier cities and aspiring nations. No longer are candidates bidding for events in order to showcase existing assets only. Instead, bids are initiated to bring about a fundamental restructuring of urban environments and democratic processes. Events bids are implicated in urban masterplans in the knowledge that, if successful, awarding bodies will ensure that these commitments are delivered.

In Chapter 3, we suggested that there are at least three ways that event bids can be conceptualised – economic reframing, nation building and global positioning. It is our contention that these three conceptualisations are not mutually exclusive, but instead impact each other, depending on the political, economic and social circumstances of the prospective bidder. We posit that both the economic reframing and global positioning conceptualisations belong to the same neo-liberal entrepreneurial discourse which has intensified in recent years. The nation-building agenda cannot exist on its own without being allied to the other two conceptualisations. To make the case for an event bid on the basis of rebuilding a nation or region (as we saw with the South Africa bid for the 2010 FIFA World Cup), the candidate must present a strong economic rationale to satisfy the awarding body that it will be able to translate positive emotional capital into financial return. The awarding body's financial model is dependent on generating a windfall from its primary event assets, with the Olympic Games (IOC) or the World Cup (FIFA) being the most obvious cases. For a bid to be considered a serious contender, it cannot be viewed as a financial risk to the awarding body or, crucially, to its sponsor family. The decision of the Commonwealth Games Federation, in March 2017, to strip Durban, South Africa, of the hosting rights for the 2022 iteration of the event due to its inability to deliver on the agreed financial commitments highlights this clearly.

Significantly, we have argued that event awarding bodies and event bidding organisations are working to broadly the same market-focused and entrepreneurial agenda. So, whilst over time sporting mega event awarding bodies such as the IOC or FIFA have had to adapt their bid processes and practices to address criticisms arising from accusations of corruption, profiteering or takeover of urban environments (Müller, 2015), the direction of travel has continued to be towards the maximisation of commercial imperatives. The language of marketing and promotion permeates event bid processes, with sophisticated techniques of persuasion employed by bidders to secure the support of both internal (host population and government) and external (sponsor, awarding bodies) actors. The increasingly entrepreneurial state apparatus also participates in the consent manufacture process, providing financial and institutional resources (i.e. people and influence) to improve the chances of success. Whilst a bidding city or nation can amend its 'pitch' to satisfy local or contextual imperatives, the flexibility is always limited, as the bid process remains overly determined by an unelected and unaccountable awarding body.

Whilst it is our view that the demands of the awarding bodies continue to prevail over the interests of the prospective host, it is important to recognise some recent trends that appear to be arresting the power and influence of awarding bodies to dictate terms. First, competition for the world's most recognised sporting mega event – the Olympic Games (Summer and Winter versions) – has diminished in recent years with fewer initial applicants and more withdrawals during the bid process. The IOC has responded to this threat to its main asset by introducing reforms to its own bid processes that reduce the costs associated with bidding and remove the distinction between applicant and candidate city, meaning that all serious applicants automatically become the latter. However, the bid cycle for the 2024 Games, as it reached its climax, was increasingly troubled with late withdrawals from the bid process (Rome and Budapest) and widespread discussion of a crisis enveloping the IOC's bid cycle. Second, the involvement of law enforcement agencies (including the Federal Bureau of Investigation (FBI)) in investigating FIFA over claims of corruption within that organisation has removed the impression that awarding bodies are outside the reach of the law. As discussed in Chapter 7, being located in Switzerland has enabled the awarding bodies for sporting mega events to avoid being subject to the same legal frameworks affecting other non-profit organisations. The protection that FIFA and the IOC experienced from their extra-jurisdictional status is now being challenged. This challenge relates to another reason for the diminishing power and influence of awarding bodies. The public mood has shifted significantly over recent years, affecting the reputation of awarding bodies and threatening the longer-term commercial viability of their primary event assets. Reputational damage can be detrimental to awarding bodies as they rely heavily on the commercial value accruable from corporate sponsors willing to be associated with a positive brand proposition. Ultimately, FIFA removed its long-term leader, Sepp Blatter, because the organisation was facing pressure from sponsors, law enforcement agencies and national federations to reform.

Host bidding organisations and the democratic deficit

Whilst we recognise that greater scrutiny upon awarding bodies may lead to reform of these organisations and the bidding processes they govern, we do not see the same accountabilities affecting the behaviour of host event bidding organisations. In advanced liberal democracies, event bids continue to originate as a result of pro-growth coalitions of public and private sector actors who have a significant stake in restructuring the urban environment. Event bidding organisations are often headed up by prominent business people, subsidised by the local state and given a status that protects them from the extent of democratic scrutiny other public bodies experience, at least in the democracies of the West. The nature of the competitive event bidding process means that bid organisations are expected to operate in a 'nimble' manner, employing experts from the private sector to develop a persuasive narrative and to campaign for support internally and externally. As discussed in Chapters 3 and 6, bid organisations utilise sophisticated marketing and public relations techniques to campaign and lobby on behalf of the prospective host city or nation. A cadre of expert bid consultants is appointed, at significant cost to the subsidising public purse, to select and promote the unique assets of the place and communicate these to decision makers. Extravagant promises are made to awarding bodies and to the wider public, albeit 'normally' within the rules of the bidding game. These promises extend to long-term political commitments, sport development investment and infrastructural innovation. It is claimed that bid committees 'need' to participate in the dark arts of politicking in order to increase their likelihood of success.

In countries where democracy takes a different form, or is absent completely, event bidding organisations are even less accountable to the wider citizenry. As McGillivray & McPherson (2012) have argued, the limits of democracy apply when non-democratic governance structures enable ruling families, single party states and powerful corporate interests to secure an advantage in bidding contests. It is possible for the Qatari ruling family to 'decide' to bid for the FIFA World Cup without the need for checks and balances via the sort of parliamentary democracies found in, for example, the UK or Germany. Though the bidding process for the principal sporting events has changed to ensure indicators of public opinion and government support are accommodated, in practice, non-democratic states can relatively easily secure positive responses using state media as propaganda or by simply guaranteeing delivery of the bid book promises.

Though the bidding process for peripatetic cultural events (Chapter 4) is subject to much less critical scrutiny than for sporting mega events, the bid organisations established are similar in terms of their membership and level of accountability to the state and broader public(s). The bid process for cultural events such as the European Capital of Culture or even the UK Capital of Culture, still requires prospective hosts to create a formal bid entity that is at arm's length from the local state, whilst often being subsidised by it. We have talked at length in this text about the problems associated with the great and good, business leaders and expert consultants leading these bid organisations. We conclude here that it matters little whether the bid focus is sporting, cultural or even business oriented. Central to their *raison d'être* is to operate as autonomous business units and bid for contracts – only the contract in this case rarely carries with it a pot of gold to reinvest in other activities. Instead, the contract ties the event bidding organisation and its successor delivery body into significant cost outlays that can have long-term impacts on the state of public finances in a local and/or national state context.

Event bidding: contesting the circus

We have argued that event bidding processes and associated rules and conventions produce behaviours on behalf of awarding bodies and bid organisations that can compromise the rule of law, democratic principles and ethical standards. The main awarding bodies discussed throughout this book – the IOC and FIFA – originate from private gentlemen's clubs in the nineteenth century, and there is a legacy to their constitution and governance arrangements that protects them from the sort of scrutiny that is commonplace for other organisations. The special status that these organisations have enjoyed over the last century has enabled impropriety to flourish, predominantly because they have been able to design and implement their own rules that operate outside the boundaries of national territories and jurisdictions.

However, we have shown that over the last few years there is evidence of opposition to event bids securing traction, both from the perspective of the host city and also from the wider public. We recognise that opposition is not something new, but it is our contention that it is more pronounced than seen in previous decades, and more effective. Whereas, since the mid-1960s opposition to sporting mega event bids has been visible, campaigns were ultimately unsuccessful in achieving their stated aim to prevent the bid from being submitted. Oppositional groups secured some marginal concessions from event bid organisations, but they invariably failed to fundamentally alter the event. However, we propose that opposition to event bids is now more mature, with organised coalitions holding bid organisations to account much earlier in the process, with carefully managed campaigns, drawing on expertise from other failed bids. Collective (global) activity draws on wider public concerns about event extravagance and turns that into clear strategies and tactics that take the debate from the abstract to the concrete and tangible. The public that ultimately pays to subsidise event bids and event delivery is now made acutely aware of the direct costs of the choice to bid, including the alternative uses of public funds. They are also urged to use their voting power to withdraw the mandate for elected officials to support bids.

Event bid organisations and their supporters do not respond meekly to the threat posed by a more organised and mature oppositional force. Rather, they are responding in at least two distinct ways. First, bid organisations are being 'forced', in the liberal democracies of the West at least, to adhere to more stringent standards around governance, financial probity and transparency in the activities of their employees. There is a need to show that they are playing by the rules, with the threat of exposure more pronounced than ever before. Second, bid organisations operate even more secretively, avoiding announcing their intentions until the very last moment and tying themselves closely to the interest of the local state and its entrepreneurial ambitions. In this case, to criticise the bid organisation and its desire to bring an event with multiple 'benefits' to the host state is viewed as a critique of the local state itself. So, bound to the interests of capital in producing economic sustenance, the local state defends its position, protecting the interests of the bid committee, reinforcing the economic reframing narrative as a result.

The future of event bidding

We conclude with some reflections on the potential state of event bidding over the course of the next decade. We have chosen this timeframe because to look any further would be unrealistic, given the nature of the political, economic and social changes witnessed over the last decade, including a global financial meltdown and the emergence of new, more pronounced geo-political crises across the globe.

1 The reform agenda: awarding bodies

Building on the trends of the last five years, awarding bodies come under increasing pressure, nationally and internationally, to reform both their organisations and the bidding processes they are responsible for. The threat of international law enforcement intervention, sponsor pressure and public damnation act as drivers for change, and the principal awarding bodies (FIFA and the IOC) accept the need for further reform and implement changes to their governance structures to bring them in line with other non-governmental organisations. Given, as we have shown previously, that awarding bodies typically impose their priorities upon candidate cities and nations, it is also to be expected that the reform agenda will reach individual bid campaigns and hosts. This has been evidenced already, in 2016, with Sochi losing the hosting rights to the 2017 Bobsleigh and Skeleton World Championships in response to alleged state-sponsored doping of athletes. In Chapter 2 we indicated that almost every new bid cycle contains a demand for a new form of legacy and impact, as the perceived power of events to deliver urban renewal amplifies. We highlighted the ways in which economic, social, cultural and sustainable agendas have all been incorporated into the bid cycle for sporting mega events in recent years. As awarding bodies come under pressure to demonstrate their own reform of governance practices, it is likely that bids which can demonstrate *transparency* and *accountability* in their own practices will secure an advantage over competitors. The decision of Calgary, Canada, to commission a full feasibility study and public consultation examining the possibility of *launching* a bid for the 2026 Winter Olympics, as opposed to consulting after announcing as has happened elsewhere in the past, is perhaps the first of many bids which will place a greater emphasis on transparency, accountability and public engagement.

2 Equality and social justice: awarding bodies

In addition to awarding bodies giving greater emphasis to the transparency of their own systems and those of prospective hosts, we also think there will be an enhanced importance given to values of human rights, sustainability, equality, citizen involvement and transparency within the bid process. This, we feel, could lead to the main sporting mega event awarding bodies returning to their philosophical roots to ensure their supranational values are enshrined more effectively in the bid process (and subsequent delivery). Though the IOC has been subjected to significant criticism for paying lip service to the guiding principles contained within its Olympic Charter, its social and educational mission continues to be relevant to the challenges facing many parts of the world. The sustainability of infrastructural and legacy plans, clear commitments to protecting human rights and the rule of law are likely to be given greater weighting over the next decade, with concomitant impacts on those who can bid for these events. Some of these trends are already evident, with the IOC announcing its intention to include a much stronger standard of human rights commitment in the bidding process for the Olympic Games than has previously been required by candidate cities.

3 The reform agenda: bidding processes

Associated with the reform agenda within the awarding bodies themselves, public pressure and a declining number of applicants, particularly from Europe, could lead to a reform of the event bidding process itself. The precise nature of the reforms is difficult to predict but it is likely to include the development of more inventive formats for events such as the FIFA World Cup, the UEFA European Championship and perhaps even the Olympic Games, as well as a renegotiation of the relationship between potential hosts and awarding bodies. The IOC's *Olympic Agenda 2020* has led to some relatively marginal changes to the bid process and eligibility to bid for the Olympic Games. However, these reforms have not quelled criticisms around the gigantism of the Olympic Games. The much publicised problems surrounding the 2024 Olympic bid cycle, and the eagerness, if not desperation of the IOC to appoint hosts to 2024 and 2028 simultaneously to alleviate these concerns has already raised the possibility of a radical reworking of Olympic financing:

> This is actually a "positive opportunity" for the bid teams in Los Angeles and Paris to extract a better deal from the IOC. After years of lopsided dealings between the IOC and the host city in which everyday people shoulder the costs while the IOC and their partners monopolize the benefits, the time is right for a relationship reboot.
>
> *(Boykoff, 2017 [online])*

We believe it is likely that there will be further debate on joint bidding for the Games, as well as discussions about appointing a limited number of regular event hosts (from each continent). These debates will be fuelled by pressure on awarding bodies to avoid subjecting potential hosts to the excessive costs associated with bidding (and delivering) these events. Beyond the Olympic Games, international sporting event formats are already evidencing change, with the 2020 UEFA European Championship being delivered across multiple event hosts (13 European cities are hosting matches) and with a new format, the 2018 European Championships, being hosted by Berlin and Glasgow and including seven disciplines in a multi-sport event. Though the FIFA World Cup has yet to change its format on the basis of the prevailing mood, with the controversial bids for both the 2018 (Russia) and 2022 (Qatar) versions, it is likely that the 2026 FIFA World Cup bid process will include reform that might include the opportunity for bids with more than one host. Whilst these reforms will be couched in the language of transparency and sustainability, it is also worth noting that they will have a valuable benefit to awarding bodies. Several sporting mega events have witnessed a considerable decline in prospective candidates entering into bidding contests. Prior to losing hosting rights, Durban was the only candidate by the conclusion of the bid process for the 2022 Commonwealth Games. The 2022 Winter Olympic Games saw only two bids, Beijing and Almaty, Kazakhstan, reach the formal host city election and, as has been chronicled here, the 2024 Summer Olympic Games bid process has been fraught with protest and withdrawals. The reformation of bidding processes will undoubtedly enable a regeneration of the pool of prospective candidates for major events. Smaller nations dominated by larger cities will be increasingly able to engage with sporting mega events in a way that would not previously have been possible. The aforementioned host cities for the 2020 UEFA European Championship represent a prime example, with nations such as Azerbaijan, Ireland, Romania and Scotland all given a share of the hosting rights for an event which would otherwise be beyond their individual technical competency. A similar reformation of the bid process for the Olympic Games or FIFA World Cup will enable the IOC and FIFA to tap into a similar source of new hosts, rejuvenating their competition for future iterations of their events.

4 Professionalisation of opposition

We expect to see awarding bodies having to adhere to international standards around transparency and accountability in their operations and we also expect them, and bid organisations, to face even greater public scrutiny from what we call a *professionalisation of opposition*. Whilst we do not believe that cities or nations will simply stand back and relent from bidding for major sporting, cultural or business events, we do expect them to be more reticent to do so, should they think that their bid will be subject to detailed scrutiny and critique internally. We think the trends identified in the earlier parts of this book will simply intensify as opposition to major event bids moves from the fringes to the mainstream. Articulations of opposition will be more easily communicated, earlier in the process, via increasingly networked publics that have sophisticated understandings of how mainstream and new media can work together.

Though we forecast that the professionalisation of opposition will be a force for good in subjecting event bids to necessary scrutiny, we also recognise that unintended consequences may arise. We think there are two likely alternative possibilities. First, bid committees and their members will be even more secretive in their early deliberations, making sure they have significant political support and strong press and media relations expertise before announcing their bids – to avoid them stalling before they even get started. Second, whilst cities or nations with democratic systems withdraw or decide not to even contemplate a bid, their non-democratic international counterparts will be more likely to bid for events in the knowledge that their chances of success against advanced liberal democracies are enhanced. This suggests that in the coming years we will see a continuation of the recent south-east turn which has seen an increasing number of peripatetic events awards to cities in the nations of the Southern and Eastern hemispheres, posing a significant challenge for the Northern and Western nations, which have traditionally dominated the hosting of these events. Therefore, in the face of increasingly professionalised opposition and fiercer global competition for hosting rights, we believe that there will be a further professionalisation of the bid process. Already, we are seeing a more nuanced understanding of the role of marketing and public relations in communicating event bid narratives. Similarly, the emergence of a global circuit of 'bid gurus' directing campaign strategies means that bid organisations are spending increasingly significant resources on hiring specialist agencies to devise bid messages to promote bids. It is our belief that this trend will grow further and infiltrate every aspect of bid campaigns for sporting and cultural events at national and international levels.

Concluding comments

We began this book by outlining the need for a sustained critique and discussion of event bidding. We argued at the outset that given the size, scale and reach of bid campaigns, greater attention needed to be paid to the *politics* of bidding, the acts of *persuasion* used to solicit support and manufacture consent for bids and the growing *resistance* to such activity caused by a range of governance and ethical issues. As we conclude, we have laid out a range of critical issues which we believe will dominate the world of bidding in the coming years. The next decade promises to be one of significant upheaval for both awarding bodies and prospective hosts. Bid cycles will be increasingly scrutinised, and activity, both by those bidding and those protesting, evermore professionalised. In this world it is little surprise that the Candidate Process for the 2024 Olympic Games was the first sporting mega event campaign to cost a cumulative $1 billion across the entire field of candidates, though it is unlikely to be the last. The coming decade promises to see a profound amplification of the issues discussed here. We conclude our text by calling for a *continued* critique of the world of event bidding.

References

Brenner, N. (2009) What is critical urban theory? *City*, 13(2–3), pp.198–207.

Boykoff, J. (2017) It's time for the International Olympic Committee to step up and pay its fair share. Available at http://www.latimes.com/sports/olympics/la-sp-oly-ioc-commentary-20170322-story.html?curator=SportsREDEF (accessed 27 March 2017).

Broudehoux, A-M. and Sánchez, F. (2015) The politics of mega event planning in Rio de Janeiro: Contesting the Olympic City of exception. In V. Viehoff and G. Poynter (eds), *Mega-event cities: Urban legacies of global sports events* (pp.109–122). London: Routledge.

McGillivray, D. and McPherson, G. (2012) 'Surfing a wave of change': A critical appraisal of the London 2012 cultural programme. *Journal of Policy Research in Tourism, Leisure & Events*, 4(2), pp.123–137.

Müller, M. (2015) The mega-event syndrome: Why so much goes wrong in mega-event planning and what to do about it. *Journal of the American Planning Association*, 81(1), pp.6–17.

INDEX